BALLERINA

PORTRAITS AND IMPRESSIONS OF NADIA NERINA

EDITED BY CLEMENT CRISP
DESIGNED BY BARNEY WAN

Weidenfeld & Nicolson

11 St John's Hill
London SW 11 1XA

Filmset by Keyspools Ltd, Golborne, Lancs

Printed in England by Westerham Press Limited, Westerham, Kent

ISBN 0 297 76951 0

CONTENTS

INTRODUCTION

The dancer's career is the saddest because the shortest in span. Tamara Karsavina called dancers 'butterflies of a brief summer' and this phrase sums up everything of the evanescence of a career that can end before middle age sets in. The life is a ceaselessly taxing round of class and rehearsal, a daily battle to surmount the body's inadequacies and a constant search for what must be an unattainable physical ideal – no dancer is ever satisfied, no dancer ever wants to rest on whatever laurels have been so hard-won. On the last day of a career, as on the first, the morning ritual of class will make the utmost demands on the physical instrument as well as on the marvellous possibilities implicit in the classic dance. There are joys, of course: rewards from achievement and from the gratitude of audiences, but these can be seen as the incidentals to the greater achievements of the company to whose service the dancer's first loyalty always seems to go.

The Royal Ballet is a company based upon the foundation of the classic academic dance, and Dame Ninette de Valois' comments upon this and upon the formation of classic dancers will be found in the text. Her own achievement in building a classic company – a task in which she was doubly blessed by the collaboration of Frederick Ashton as choreographer and Constant Lambert as musical and artistic counsellor – is massive, but equally important is not only the company she founded but also the school which has shown itself able to continue producing dancers to sustain the classic repertory. That this system is right has been proved by its fruitfulness: great dancers and great choreography have sprung from it, and the creation of a repertory, continuing and developing this classic tradition through a wealth of fine ballets, is testimony to the vitality of classicism itself, and its organic growth.

Nadia Nerina's career spanned twenty-three years in the history of the Royal Ballet; from promising young soloist to world-acclaimed ballerina, her participation in the exciting period of the company's post-war expansion is charted in this book. Like the company itself, Nerina came of age and proved herself at the Royal Opera House, Covent Garden; her roles reflect the range of the repertory, from the standard Russian classics and the Folkine masterpieces to the creation of an English masterpiece, *La Fille Mal Gardée*, and the development of a native tradition and style in the works of Ashton, Cranko and MacMillan.

Nadia Nerina's dancing excited by its physical integrity and by the completeness of its involvement with a role: there was nothing half-hearted or polite in its outline, no indecision or blurring in its effects. The full stretch of movement, the 'open' style, spoke of an artist who found the truth of an interpretation by essentially dynamic means. Grateful memories of her Aurora, or Lise, or Odette/Odile are of a physique generous and brilliant in expression. Nerina's dancing was exciting to watch because her body was never dull; its shape was taut, clearly defined, the pulse of its energies quick and sure. She was a dancer to whom the word 'virtuoso' was often applied, yet there is some slight connotation of superficial bravura in the epithet which was less than the truth about Nerina's interpretations. Her dancing could boast all those qualities of darting, impetuous speed, of dizzying turns, of sparkling foot-work that the virtuoso must possess; but this was only part of much more sensitive command of her body, which enabled her to develop her characterisations in purely physical terms. The preparation of any major role was a matter of finding the correct physical and dynamic imagery, not of making a dutiful appliqué of dramatic gesture upon a basic and unvarying manner.

G.B.L. WILSON

Her Aurora shone with youthful grace, her Odette grieved, and the drama was found within the dance itself, not outside it. Her Lise laughed in her dancing because, in fact, the dancing itself had just that happiness of a girl delightfully, ecstatically in love.

Through Nerina's own comments and those of the creators with whom she worked I have hoped to assemble testimony not just to her career – she is the least insistent of people on her own attainment – but to throw some light upon the working life of a dancer as it reflects the expansion and nature of the great national company which she served with such distinction.

The dancer's life is one in which a mysterious balance is established between athleticism and art. Without the exhausting labours of classroom and rehearsal, the dancer is nothing; without the challenge of interpretation and the creation of an artistic effect, the dancer remains an athlete. Mastery of the body is the eternal quest, but equally important is the placing of that mastery at the service of a role – be it Swan Queen or a character in a plotless ballet. Both these aspects of dancing have to be united to the best of the dancer's ability and this implies a mental concentration quite as intense as the physical effort. This is the professional secret, the inner core of the dancer's art; it is a recurrent theme in this book, and if it finds some illumination from pictures and text then my labours have not been in vain.

Clement Crisp

ACKNOWLEDGEMENTS

Thanks are due to many people who have contributed to the compilation of this book. Firstly to Nadia Nerina herself: I must record with gratitude the many happy conversations we had during the early summer of last year – conversations which, like those of other contributors to the book, I have preserved as they were spoken on to a tape recorder. The resultant immediacy of recollection and comment will, I hope, illuminate more sharply the matter of the book.

Contributors gave most generously of their precious time: without the kindness of Dame Ninette de Valois and Margaret Dale, of Eileen Keegan and Sir Robert Helpmann, of David Blair and Alexis Rassine and Kenneth MacMillan, my editorial task would have been impossible. Dame Peggy van Praagh found time to write from Australia, Arnold Haskell sent testimony of his thirty years of friendship with Nerina; Leo Kersley was most generous both in contributions and in suggestions of help. I, like everyone who writes on ballet in Russia, owe a special debt of gratitude to Mme Natalya Roslavleva in Moscow, who not only contributed her own recollections but spoke to the illustrious Marina Semyonova, and also visited Leningrad to see those great artists of the Kirov Ballet, Natalya Dudinskaya and Konstantin Sergueyev who also were kind enough to write for me. To Miss Iris Smith of the Novosti Press Agency in London I must acknowledge grateful thanks for her work in connection with these Russian friends.

To the photographers – Anthony Crickmay, Alan Cunliffe, Zoe Dominic, and to Mrs Brenda Rogers who was most generous in providing the pictures taken by her husband, the late Houston Rogers – I owe a great debt of gratitude.

Even more special thanks must go to G.B.L. Wilson whose photographic record of the past three decades of British ballet is a unique and wonderful source for marvellously apt pictures. Mr Boris Skidelsky of the archives at the Royal Opera House, Covent Garden, gave up valuable time to look for pictures, and to photographers not otherwise mentioned, thanks are also due. To the various critics and writers whose words I have quoted go grateful thanks: especially to Miss Mary Clarke of *The Dancing Times*, Mr Peter Williams of *Dance and Dancers*, Mr Eric Johns of *The Stage*, Mr Clive Barnes of *The New York Times*, and to my colleague on *The Financial Times*, Andrew Porter, from all of whom lengthier quotations have proved of particular relevance to particular ballets. To all other writers from whom I have taken quotes, equally grateful acknowledgement is made. Miss Rosemary Gray gave much help; the assistance offered by Miss Gay Burdett and Mr Max Fairbrother to Barney Wan and myself has been invaluable; and as always I must offer an especial thankyou to Miss Carol Venn for her speed, accuracy, and her real help with typing and preparation of the manuscript. Finally, this book owes much to the kindness and help given by Miss Ann Wilson of Weidenfeld and Nicolson.

CC

SOUTH AFRICAN CHILDHOOD

Though it may no longer be possible to speak of an Empire, the fact remains that the Royal Ballet owes a great deal to the contribution made by dancers from what was the British Commonwealth and Empire. The pioneering spirit that took Anna Pavlova round the world, from capital cities to remote townships with the most rudimentary of stages, spread a seed of ballet that bore remarkable fruit – one celebrated example is the inspiration she gave the young Frederick Ashton in Lima, Peru. The touring Ballets Russes ensembles of the thirties were a further stimulus to audiences the world over; teaching organisations like the Royal Academy of Dancing and the Cecchetti Society encouraged and nurtured young talent in the then British Empire. The result of all this activity and interest became particularly noticeable immediately the war was over: dozens of young dancers realised their ambition to come to London to study and dance with the Sadler's Wells Ballet – among them Rowena Jackson and Alexander Grant from New Zealand, Elaine Fifield from Australia, Nadia Nerina, Maryon Lane, David Poole and John Cranko from South Africa. It may be that the need to travel great distances to pursue a dancing career marked a seriousness of intention among these young performers; certainly, their gifts were quickly appreciated by the company they joined. The tradition thus established has been maintained ever since: the number of artists in the Royal Ballet and students from the Commonwealth in the Royal Ballet School is testimony to the continuing importance and vitality of this link. CC

The first time I ever went on stage was in South Africa in an opera. A touring company brought a production of *Madam Butterfly* to Bloemfontein and they wanted someone for Cio-Cio San's baby. Although I was eight or nine years old, I was tiny, so I was chosen, though I must have been rather heavy for the singer who had to carry me. I was dressed in a little Japanese costume, and set down on a mat with my back to the audience – where I remained absolutely fascinated by the soprano. When she killed herself with a dagger, I burst into tears, believing she was dead – and no one could console me. The next night there she was again to carry me on – I was most puzzled, and could not understand how she had not hurt herself terribly the night before. *NN*

Acrobatic solo: the costume was white and silver and I was ten years old.

I was born in Cape Town, South Africa. My father was a businessman and my parents had no connection with either the theatre or ballet. Together with my younger brother Lee, we lived in Bloemfontein – a semi-desert town. When I was eight years old I twisted my ankle and our doctor advised that I be sent to dancing classes to strengthen it. The exercises were painful and difficult and I would rather have been at the swimming pool – the only inducement to my going was being allowed to eat a pomegranate off the tree after the class. Even so, my teacher seemed to recognise that I had unusual ability for she insisted that I continued my training.

Shortly before the war we moved to Durban where I was sent to two quite exceptional teachers, Eileen Keegan and Dorothea McNair. Eileen Keegan had danced professionally with the Pavlova Company. She was, and still is, a very serious person and a most dedicated teacher. Her approach to dancing was neither a ritual nor in any way pretentious, although she instilled into us an absolute respect for the ballet. She impressed upon us that we should always regard the stage as a very special place and that artists had devoted their lives to performing on it. She explained that if one was fortunate enough to have some ability one should have respect for one's gift, but if one wished to add something of one's own to the theatre or ballet as an artist, however naturally talented, it would need discipline, hard work and dedication. Nothing would just 'come'. Eileen Keegan's teaching had a profound influence on my career.

Dorothea McNair, a vital and expressive person, had studied and worked with Dame Marie Rambert. She was also a brilliant classical mime artist and a born teacher. The combination of these two outstanding personalities in one studio was unique and the standard of training, I now realise, was extraordinarily high.

During the war my father became the Government motor controller and we moved to Johannesburg. The wrench at leaving the studio was enormous and after a few months I virtually ran away from home to get back to classes in Durban. Miss Keegan and Miss McNair realised my determination and finally persuaded my parents to let me stay. The problem was my general education, as no boarding school would permit a student time off for ballet training. Eventually, however, special arrangements were made for me to continue my general education at the drama school run by Elizabeth Sneddon, an eminent professor and lecturer at the Durban University. This satisfied my parents and the requirements of the educational authorities.

These days were long and marvellous – filled with work. I would get up at 6.30 am and it was odd to see the other girls going to school while I stood in the garden among the paw-paw trees working on voice production and breath control – excellent training for a dancer. Even now I can easily swim the length of a swimming pool underwater. I would arrive at the dancing school

Left In *The Seekers*. **Opposite** Eileen Keegan's production of *The Seekers*.

Nadia came to me in Durban as a pupil in 1939 – and my first memory of her is of hard work – sh used to be in the studio by 9.00 in the morning and was never still for a moment. She had a ver pliable body and a strong technique, and she was exciting to teach, always working very hard o any physical problem. It was not just a question of coming to class twice a day, but the though Nadia put into her dancing, how she took corrections and worked on them. Dorothea McNai and I did as many shows as we could for our students and in *The Seekers* I thought Nadia wa absolutely magnificent. She had a Russian quality – a lovely jump – and she gave a great deal i performance. Even as a student Nadia was an exciting dancer.

Eileen Keega

at 9 o'clock for an hour and a half of practising on my own before joining the regular ballet class, and this was followed by an hour's work with Elizabeth Sneddon. We always spent the lunch-hour at concerts in the City Hall and afterwards I would dash off for a further two hours' study at the Drama School before finally attending the character class at the dance studio. That – and I find it hard to believe now – was my regular daily routine.

In the midst of this intensive training my mother died suddenly and my father wisely advised that I return to Durban and carry on with my ballet training and studies. The deep shock of my mother's death made me become even more intensely involved in my work, and I entered for every section in the forthcoming Drama Festival. I was amazed to discover that not only had I been awarded the highest marks, but I had won the £500 bursary for drama studies overseas. The decision was suddenly forced upon me to make the choice between drama or ballet as a career. Nervous exhaustion had made me ill and I was sent away into the Natal hills behind Durban to recuperate. There I decided that the challenge for me was dancing; the drama bursary happily went to a friend of mine.

My teachers had taught me all they could and persuaded my father how important it was for me to go to Europe to start my career. I was now sixteen and I had read that Beryl Grey, who was a year my senior, was already dancing leading roles in London. Time was slipping by, and I saw myself getting too old! I went to Cape Town to wait for a boat. While I was there I went to classes at the University Ballet under the direction of Dulcie Howes and renewed my acquaintance with John Cranko whom I had known briefly in Johannesburg. He bubbled with ideas and had a fantastic imagination and even then was clearly enormously talented.

The war was only just over and it was extremely difficult to get on a ship, but my father eventually managed to arrange a passage and in October 1945, seventeen years old, I set sail for England.

NN

NN ACUTT

WITH SADLER'S WELLS

The six years of the Second World War could have proved fatal for ballet in Britain, yet the bombings, the call-up of male dancers (Bernard Shaw urged that they should be exempt; the government rightly felt otherwise), and shortages of all sorts of necessary materials were miraculously surmounted. The Sadler's Wells Ballet, of necessity, toured throughout the country and built an audience and a reputation that it was never again to lose. A 'ballet-boom' started that lasted well into the 1950s – explicable only in part by the public's desire for theatrical excitement and glamour in a time of austerity – and with its unexpected promotion to the Covent Garden stage, the Sadler's Wells Ballet showed itself strong and talented enough to benefit from its great opportunity. After the war major visiting companies – American Ballet Theatre, Les Ballets des Champs Elysées, the de Basil Ballets Russes – were soon seen in London; though we might admire the American's vitality and the elegance of the French, and regret that the Ballets Russes was but a ghost of its former self, the maturity and distinction of the Sadler's Wells troupe was plain for all to see. We had a truly national company, one with a healthy tradition of creativity and training, an ensemble rightly to be shown in an opera house. But the parent theatre at Sadler's Wells could not be left ungratefully empty, and the formation of the Sadler's Wells Theatre Ballet under Dame Peggy Van Praagh's guidance provided a nursery for young dancers and young choreographers; from it came much of the new talent – Cranko and MacMillan, Fifield, Lane, Nerina, Blair and how many more – that was in time to feed the main company at Covent Garden.

CC

Ann Negus as the Fairy of the Woodland Glades.
The nurse standing on the left of the cradle is Nadia Nerina: first performance of *The Sleeping Beauty* at the Royal Opera House, 1946.

ARRIVAL IN ENGLAND

I arrived at Southampton in November 1945 in the middle of a terrible fog. All I can remember of the journey to London are the endless chimney pots. I went straight to the Mercury Theatre to see Marie Rambert because Dorothea McNair, who had worked with her, had written saying that I was arriving. I was taken in to see Madame Rambert and the first thing she told me to do was to take off my coat and stretch my foot – I felt like a prize pony. Then I was whipped into class and afterwards Madame Rambert wanted to know where I was staying, and out of the blue, asked me to stay in her house as her guest, which was extraordinarily kind. One other remarkable thing happened that morning. Just before I went into class Madame Rambert asked my age, and I said I was seventeen, quite unthinkingly. 'What a shame,' she said, 'if you were a year older you could join the company and come on tour with us to Germany.' I was speechless with shyness and did not tell her that I had just turned eighteen: my shyness was really a trick of fate – it meant that my future was to be with another company.

The school at the Mercury Theatre was quite unfamiliar to me; I had never seen a professional class and there were all the Rambert dancers in the ragged leg-warmers and woollies that real dancers wear in class: superb artists like Sally Gilmour and Paula Hinton and Joyce Graeme. That same day Madame Rambert gave me a room at the top of her house – I had never seen such a tall house in my life. The room had a gas fire which, although I was freezing, I never dared put on because the gas 'popped' when you lit it, and I was terrified of it. Before my daily class I would arrive at the Mercury Theatre at 8.30 in the morning and work for an hour and a half by myself; it made me feel less homesick – it was the time in South Africa when my friends would be taking their morning class and I was with them in spirit. The ballet room was always hot and stuffy when I arrived because the stove had been stoked up and all the windows closed, so I would open them at once. When the Rambert dancers arrived I would be warm but the room would be freezing. They soon put a stop to that!

Madame Rambert took a very kind interest in me. She used to work with me and use the most graphic expressions – very sharp ones, too, like 'Your fingers are just a bunch of bananas' or 'Don't stand like that, you look pregnant'.

Then I started to go to classes given by Stanislas Idzikovski in a nearby studio. There, someone told me that I ought to go to the Sadler's Wells. I was very happy at the thought of extra training and so it was arranged for me to go. Class was being held in a huge room with a grand piano and about twenty students in immaculate white practice dress. They looked like angels to me, and reminded me of class in South Africa – very different from the sheer professionalism and odds and ends of woollies that I saw at the Rambert school. Then it was pointed out to me that I simply could not attend both schools. I would have to make a decision.

In the meantime Madame Rambert took me to see my first professional ballet performance – her company was appearing at the Lyric, Hammersmith, in a matinee of *Peter and the Wolf*, *Giselle* Act II and *Dark Elegies*. I can still remember how puzzled I was by the classical mime of the Queen of the Wilis (the 'Here-you-die' passage) and how disappointed I was by it. But I recall how profoundly impressed I was by *Dark Elegies*, so much so that I hid under a seat in the theatre to stay and see the evening performance. Even now one of my great regrets is that I never worked with Antony Tudor; *Elegies* moved me totally.

Then I received a letter from my father; he had been advised in South Africa that I should join the Wells Company if I could, and after Christmas I had to tell Madame Rambert that I was going to leave her school. I was very upset, because she had been incredibly good to me, but my father then sent me a cable saying that it was an 'order' for me to go to the Wells, and go to the Wells I did. There I found to my dismay that I was not in class with the white angels I had seen at first (they, I discovered later, were the cream of the school, being groomed for the new junior company) and not even in the spacious studio, but in a dark room with a few indifferent students, or so it seemed to me. I was in despair. I felt fat and sluggish after spending a lazy Christmas with relatives in Worthing, and one evening in desperation to lose weight, I took a large dose of Glauber salts followed by a roastingly hot bath.

The next morning I could not open my eyes as my face was so swollen, nor could I stagger out of bed. I had the worst case of measles it is possible to have, and – because I had recently been in the class laden with germs – this news threw the Wells into a terrible tizzy. They feared I might have given the measles to the white angels who were then being prepared for the opening of the junior company to be called the Sadlers Wells Theatre Ballet. After six weeks, I was overjoyed when I was called as an extra to appear in the prologue of *The Sleeping Beauty* for the historic opening night of the Sadler's Wells Company at the Royal Opera House, Covent Garden, on 20 February 1946. I was one of the two little nurses who stood beside Aurora's cradle. However, the newly formed Sadler's Wells Theatre Ballet at the Sadler's Wells Theatre under the direction of Peggy Van Praagh was then rehearsing for their first tour of the provinces, so I was promptly returned to the junior company as a full member.

We must have been a handful, all teenagers and very bubbly. Among my friends were Anne Heaton, Sheilah O'Reilly, Donald Britton, Leo Kersley, Kenneth MacMillan, Peter Darrell and John Cranko. I remember one night in Bath the boys went across from the theatre to a pub to sample the cider and the resulting performance was rather chaotic. On another fine early summer day we went swimming and got sunburned; Peggy Van Praagh was aghast with us in *Les Sylphides* – all lobster red and smothered in wet-white!

It was on this tour in Bath that I had my first notice – for the little waltz in *Les Sylphides* – and my first bouquet, from Arnold Haskell's mother, who told him about 'this young Russian who looks like Lopokova'.

That year I went to Paris in the holidays to study each day with Preobrazhenska. She was like a bird, and had genius as a teacher. The following year Elaine Fifield (who was my contemporary) joined me and for several weeks we went together to Preobrazhenska. It was fun because we were both the same size and we could work fascinating swaps with our clothes to make it seem as if we had vast wardrobes – which we hadn't! And Preobrazhenska taught me the pas de trois solo in *Swan Lake* which had been one of her roles in St Petersburg fifty years before. *NN*

The Circus Dancer in *Mardi Gras*, with choreography by Andrée Howard: first staged by Sadler's Wells Theatre Ballet in November 1946.

MARDI GRAS

All I remember now is my very blonde wig, and three of the boys who danced in the ballet: John Cranko, Kenneth MacMillan and Peter Darrell.

I was put into the first cast quite suddenly and I had to learn a lot of new choreography. I found it very difficult, because I was not then used to learning quickly. Andrée Howard did not seem particularly pleased that I had been given the first performance and there were some unfinished bits of the choreography which terrified me. I shall never forget rehearsing in the top studio at the Wells when everyone else had gone home, with the fireman (on whose shoulder I used to cry) sitting there, asking him if he thought this looked right, or if that looked better. On the first night I was very, very nervous. There were some extraordinary turns at the end of my solo which I had to make up, but as it turned out Andrée Howard was very pleased. *NN*

MARDI GRAS

Perhaps it will not be out of place here to welcome to our English company three young South Africans, John Cranko, Pamela Chrimes and Nadia Nerina who appear in this ballet.

– Richard Buckle – *Ballet*, December 1946

My earliest recollection of Nadia is of a vivacious teenager who arrived for class at Rosebery Avenue from South Africa, shortly after the formation of the Sadler's Wells Theatre Ballet. She had a happy face and was full of energy and enthusiasm, qualities she shared with another South African, John Cranko.

I had a special interest in Nadia as she was a pupil of Eileen Keegan who, with her sister, had been a fellow-student of mine at Margaret Craske's school in London, where the Cecchetti method was taught. The Keegan sisters had opened a school in South Africa, and had given Nadia a strong technical grounding. Nadia's bright personality and strong technique were exploited by Andrée Howard in the role of the circus dancer in her ballet *Mardi Gras*. Nadia had a great success in this role, which established her immediately with the British public.

It was most interesting for me to note that Frederick Ashton used these same qualities when he created the role of Lise for her in *La Fille Mal Gardée* in 1960. He also made great use of her lovely light jump, always a pleasing quality in a dancer. By this time Nadia had developed into a fine artist and ballerina, but her strong, clear technique and bubbling personality remained for me her greatest assets. Dame Peggy Van Praagh

Sheilah O'Reilly and Nadia Nerina in *Bailemos*: choreography by Celia Franca.

No matter how small a role may be, it is important; I feel it is the role that one must respect, not the artist dancing it. Conversely, I always had great respect for whoever was dancing a part because of the skill they had acquired to do it well. It is never a question of just doing the steps; of course you must be able to do them, but there is nothing special about 'getting through' a role. This was something I realised from my very earliest days in the company, something Madam got across both to her dancers and her audience. I remember how important it seemed even to be third cast in a role; eventually you landed up dancing it at a Saturday matinée – and that, you felt, was fantastic. *NN*

Les Sylphides with Leo Kersley.

Above John Cranko's first ballet in England was *Children's Corner* performed at the New Theatre in 1946 by the Royal Academy of Dancing Production Club: Nadia Nerina and David Poole.
Below *Le Carnaval* staged by Sadler's Wells Theatre Ballet: Nadia Nerina as Papillon and John Cranko as Pierrot.

MOVING TO COVENT GARDEN

Dame Ninette de Valois

Towards the end of the war, when I thought about the future I imagined that after all our war-time touring and our London seasons we should be sent off again on some immense tour, tucked away out of sight, while there would be an avalanche of Russian and other ballet companies. Suddenly we found ourselves at Covent Garden, entrusted with keeping it open while an opera company was formed. This was a matter of great significance to us, and yet I had never imagined that it could ever happen. People may talk about their great plans, but I do not feel that one really plans very much. Things just happen; one thing leads to another, and it is absolute pomposity for anyone to claim that they have planned everything. But you do have to be sharp enough to see which plan you must follow. You may make a big mistake and pick the wrong opportunity, but the all-over plan is laid out for you by circumstances. Look what the war did for us! Opening the Royal Opera House was immensely significant, and we filled it every night for a month with *The Sleeping Beauty*; people were almost reluctant for us to get on with the next programme. Of course, life in Britain was very austere; with rationing and no cars and nothing to spend money on, the theatre flourished, and the stalls at the Opera House only cost fifteen shillings. I was given the weekly box-office returns – capacity at Covent Garden was exactly £7000 and that figure came in, absolutely exact, week after week. I got quite sick of it! Just after the war was a good time for artists, because you could feel secure, and therefore live and think like artists. It was, on those terms, a wonderful time.

The state opening of the Royal Opera House, Covent Garden, after the war – the Sadler's Wells Ballet in *The Sleeping Beauty*, 20 February 1946.

JOINING THE SENIOR COMPANY

In December 1947 I was transferred to the senior Sadler's Wells Company at Covent Garden and within three days I was dancing the mazurka in *Les Sylphides* with Alexis Rassine, one of the principal dancers of the Covent Garden company. This was undreamed of promotion, but was followed by proper grounding in the corps de ballet. I had never danced in a corps de ballet before. The other members of the corps did not take too kindly to the young girl who had been doing solos with the Theatre Ballet, and who had immediately danced the lead in *Sylphides* with Rassine, and who was now floundering about as a swan. They must have thought I needed taking down a peg or two, and they did so; the corps de ballet was superb and I did not know anything about the repertory – so if I whispered during a performance 'which way do I turn?' someone would say 'find out'. It was terrifying on the big stage, and I used to cry most nights. Suddenly, however, the girls realised that I was petrified and they became marvellously helpful to me.

I was soon given the part of understudy in the *Lac* pas de trois –

just the role that Preobrazhenska had taught me; she had told me that when she made her entrance she would be very charming to all the courtiers, as if she were saying 'How do you do', 'How do you do', with a lot of personal touches, and she showed me exactly how she had done it. When I did this in rehearsal Madam (Ninette de Valois) told me very sharply 'Child, you were not taught to do that. Do it the way you were shown'. Quite rightly, she wanted it done in the company style, without the bird-like grace and nuances that Preobrazhenska had taught me. I realised that I was the most junior person in the company and I must do exactly what I was told, but eventually I was given the solo in a performance. I threw caution to the winds and did it as Preobrazhenska had shown me – and Madam was delighted. Shortly after that I was made first cast: Madam realised that it was my style, and she was always wonderful in correcting, helping and encouraging my natural style. *NN*

HOUSTON ROGERS

Mam'zelle Angot, one of Massine's revivals for Covent Garden.

DANCERS AFTER THE WAR

Dame Ninette de Valois

Soon after the war was over I think that, technically speaking, we were able to up-grade the Royal Ballet schooling. In the theatre our own dancers had many more opportunities for working and developing; we also had a lot of young dancers coming to join us from the Commonwealth, and they gradually helped to strengthen our ranks. Nerina was one of these, and quite soon it was obvious where her talents lay; it was only a question of time before she would prove herself.

The influx of dancers also meant that we had many different types of dancer, our own Fonteyn, May and Shearer and Grey, then Nerina and Jackson from the Commonwealth, and Elvin from Russia. The variety of type was enormous and they all stressed something very special in the classical work. I am sure that one of the two specially strong points in Nadia Nerina's work was her fine elevation, which is not a strong point with English dancers generally, and this highlight of hers was an incentive to other dancers with the same possibility there, just as with Rowena Jackson it was her pirouettes. These artists are important for just such reasons. Also, Nadia had a lovely natural flow of movement. Like all the Commonwealth girls she was a hard-worker; so, of course, were our English girls, and we must not forget their difficulties after years of diet problems during the long war behind them. The Commonwealth artists joined us after an upbringing that knew of sunshine, security and good food, and our artists went into Covent Garden at the opposite end of the scale. But I do not think that we would have succeeded without the help of the Commonwealth! We set the example; the Commonwealth gave us its most talented dancers.

Cinderella to Prokofiev's music was Sir Frederick Ashton's first full-length ballet: staged at the Royal Opera House in December 1948. The Spring Fairy was the first role Ashton created for Nadia Nerina.

FAIRY SPRING

The first time I worked with Ashton was in *Cinderella* in 1948. It was an awful November day in a basement in Kingsway. I was very young and in awe of him as our greatest choreographer. I remember Hilda Gaunt playing the music of the Spring Fairy in this dingy hall, and when she finished, Ashton said, 'Well, what does it sound like, your Fairy Spring?' I said, 'Bursting of buds' and Ashton announced, 'Right, that's what we'll do', and that is how the solo started, and why the little jumps and the hand movements are as they are.

NN

ROGER WOOD

Cinderella.

MAJOR ROLES

In the classics I believe that the entrance before a solo or pas de deux is of the utmost importance. It is the ability to walk on and stand perfectly still, with an inner composure before commencing to dance, which gives the artist authority. The full-length classical ballets are an enormous responsibility for the performer, far greater than dancing three short ballets in an evening. It is more than a question of stamina; it is one of emotion, of keeping an interpretation running through an entire evening. Responsibility to the company is equally important, and you have to set the tone for a performance as leading dancer. If you light up the Rose Adagio, the whole act and the whole company benefit; your fellow artists are dependent on you as the focus of the work; they know every step, and if you muff something you are letting *them* down. Though the physical effort is tremendous, the real reward is this responsibility. The involvement, the thrill of leading a performance, cannot be experienced in any other way, and the release of this sustained tension comes with the applause at the end of the ballet. I realised this especially after working on television, where there is no applause after a performance; I found that it could sometimes take me several days to unwind after a TV appearance.

With classical roles the dancer knows the story and will have seen the ballet performed many times; the choreography is familiar – over the years the roles have been passed down from one dancer to another. Naturally, by the time I came to dance the classics I had formed my own ideas of how I would interpret them.

But, creating a new role, like Lise in *La Fille Mal Gardée*, is entirely different. One works with the choreographer while the ballet is developing and there is a satisfying feeling that one has helped to formulate a new character.

During my career I danced all the great classics very many times but I never tired of interpreting each of these complex heroines, because however many times I danced them I continually found that there was something new to say. *NN*

Moira Shearer first danced the title role in Ashton's *Cinderella*. When she fell ill in March 1951 Nadia Nerina took over the role.

I think that the most difficult thing I ever had to learn was just to walk on stage and stand still. I remember that when I was given a leading role, I automatically put my chin up as I went on stage. I knew that one had to have 'presence', and when you are young the only way you think of doing this is to raise your head and say 'Here I am'. But with experience, you relax, you do not have to *make* that presence any more – you have, I suppose, acquired it.

NN

HOUSTON ROGERS

'An adorable spontaneity' (*The Observer*).

Coronation night 1953.

The Sadler's Wells Ballet celebrated the coronation of Queen Elizabeth with Ashton's specially choreographed *Homage to the Queen.* The cast included Margot Fonteyn, Michael Somes, Beryl Grey, John Field, Nadia Nerina, Alexis Rassine, Violetta Elvin, John Hart and Alexander Grant.

Left In *Swan Lake* with Alexis Rassine. '. . . a fluent unruffled mastery of technique that belongs to the true ballerina.' (*The Guardian*.)
Right In Ashton's *A Wedding Bouquet* as the Bride with Alexander Grant as the Groom.

Ninette de Valois' *Don Quixote* staged in 1950 with Robert Helpmann in the title role and Margot Fonteyn as Dulcinea, Alexander Grant as Sancho Panza. Nadia Nerina was a serving wench.

ROGER WOOD

As the Can-Can dancer in Massine's *La Boutique Fantasque* – at the Edinburgh Festival, 194

Sadler's Wells' triumph in New York, 1949. *The Sleeping Beauty*: from left to right – Margaret Dale, Douglas Steuart, Violetta Elvin, Alexis Rassine, Margot Fonteyn, Constant Lambert, Ninette de Valois, Frederick Ashton, Robert Helpmann, Beryl Grey, Alexander Grant, Nadia Nerina, Kenneth MacMillan and Pamela May.

TOURING ACROSS AMERICA

The first New York season in 1949 was unforgettable; the company had an overwhelming success, and after the first-night performance of *The Sleeping Beauty* I can still remember how we were escorted through the streets by a police motorcade to a reception given for us by Mayor O'Dwyer.

Those early tours across America were very long; the second lasted six months, and out of 147 performances I danced in 145. We all travelled together – company, orchestra, stage staff, sets and costumes – on a 'Sadler's Wells Train', which had its own special time-table, and we actually lived on it for a period of six weeks when we were dancing one-night stands.

Because the train was unscheduled it never left any city before three o'clock in the morning, and we would arrive at the next city at about seven o'clock, have breakfast at the station, then get into buses and go to the theatre and rehearse all morning. Then came lunch and a chance to rest in the train or in hotel rooms that were booked for us for the day. Back to more rehearsals, then the performance, followed by the hospitality, because the Americans were immensely kind. However, you did not dare do more than sip the drinks because you had had no food since lunch and had just been dancing, and you could not relax entirely because you were asked hundreds of questions by the guests. By one o'clock in the morning you would be back at the station, looking for somewhere to have bacon and eggs. And then on to the train to sleep, even though it sometimes moved on again that night. There was a terrific camaraderie and lots of hard work. *NN*

A DANCER'S PROGRESS *Ballet Today*, November 1959

Leo Kersley, *premier danseur of The Sadler's Wells Theatre Ballet*

Because Michael Fokine has always seemed to me to be the outstanding choreographer of this century, it is perhaps only logical that my favourite dancer of the post-war generation should be Nadia Nerina. Since the days of Karsavina and Lopokova, it is hard to think of another ballerina so ideal in the Fokine roles, for Nerina is equally suitable to all three of the *Sylphides* dancers, to Columbine and Papillon; she was enchanting in *Le Spectre de la Rose* and her performances in *Firebird* and *Petrushka* finally broke down the reserve of even the most conservative of critics and won her the 'rave' notices that she has been enjoying ever since.

That there was reserve towards Nerina's work on the part of a proportion of the audience as well as the critics cannot be denied, but it can be easily explained. Nerina is the first British ballerina who is not in any way like her two great predecessors, Markova and Fonteyn. She is an outstanding example of the type which first emerged in the person of the young Baronova in the early thirties; instead of the tragic, dark, static beauty which has typified so many ballerinas, Nerina has gaiety, lightness, elevation and blonde colouring. In the thirties Baronova was the ideal instrument for the Russian choreographers, Massine, Balanchine, Fokine and Nijinska, and at that time the public was primarily interested in the modern repertory; today the accent is on the old classics, and largely because of her appearance and physical characteristics of movement, Nerina was dismissed as 'soubrette type' and it has taken many years of extremely hard work on her part to convince audiences that a classical ballerina need not *per se* be tragic and dark. Nerina is never content to pose and dramatise about the stage as a substitute for dancing; she never stops dancing for an instant and, equally important, she enjoys dancing and conveys to the audience her own passionate pleasure in what she is doing.

Here I must stress another important factor in the sudden general acceptance of Nerina's importance; the visit to London in 1956 of the Bolshoy Ballet. The Russian ballerinas, and especially Struchkova, Bogomolova and Kondratieva, brought back to the stage of Covent Garden the pleasure of perfectly controlled physical movement which Baronova and her contemporaries showed us in the thirties, and after the shouting and excitement died down, audiences and critics were in a receptive mood to appreciate the extreme physical verve and enjoyment which Nerina invariably demonstrates when she takes the stage.

Although Nerina's rise has been gradual (and how much more satisfactory that can be than to be a star overnight – and perhaps a nonentity once more three weeks later) it is still possible to note certain milestones in her career. For me, the first was when, as the Country Boy in *La Fête Etrange*, I watched her, standing beside two other 'hopefuls' in a pas de trois for three girls, perform one movement – a very high développé, taken very slowly with the supporting leg on the flat foot. Although Nerina's very nearly perfect control was strongly thrown into relief by the desperate wobbling of her companions, there was more to it than mere control. There was the beginning of the kind of wonderful inevitability in placing and timing which characterises the dancing of all great ballerinas. I shall never forget that développé – I can see it now – the beautiful delicacy of the stretched foot, the easy, unstrained arm position, the proud lift of the head and the steadiness of the supporting leg. The next milestone was her Fairy Spring in *Cinderella*. It is always hard for a young dancer to open a full-length classical ballet in the first set solo – almost as hard a task as the unfortunate Radames who has to plunge straight into 'Celeste Aida' – as countless Fairies of the Crystal Fountain can testify. Once Nerina burst into her dazzling cascade of jetés and élancé arabesques the audience's attention was riveted; she took to the vast stage as though she had been born for it, as indeed she was.

The third milestone was *Mam'zelle Angot*. If Nerina is the ideal romantic Fokine dancer, she is also admirably at home with Massine or Balanchine, and in this role (which can leave ballerinas physically sick with exhaustion), she sailed through with a touch of Struchkova's sparkle, with some of the wit of Danilova, and Baronova's technical brio – and with an ease and enjoyment borrowed from all three. What is the particular quality of Nerina's dancing which has raised her to her present position and which distinguishes her from other attractive and well-trained young dancers of the Royal Ballet? I think it is the extreme clarity of her dancing. She never blurs or softens or weakens a movement, but is always at pains to make sure that every member of the audience can see exactly what she is doing, though never how she is doing it. It is undoubtedly this quality that makes her what is known as a 'dancer's dancer'; to anyone trained in the classical technique it is a never failing delight to see a dancer using that technique with ease, pleasure and clarity. I remember, to give only one example, Lopokova breaking into the conventional *Sylphides* silence to clap enthusiastically after Nerina had danced the waltz in Cambridge in 1948. 'I don't care,' she declared, when hushed by the purists. '*I* know how difficult it is.'

In March 1954 the Sadler's Wells Ballet staged a new production of *Coppélia* by Ninette de Valois. Frederick Ashton was Coppélius, Nadia Nerina was Swanilda, and David Blair was Franz. Scenery and costumes were by Osbert Lancaster.

HOUSTON ROGERS

COPPÉLIA

Nadia Nerina is a born Swanilda. At last she has recapture the charm and sparkle she revealed so abundantly in the Theatr Ballet. . . . This Swanilda has wit instead of the dreadful pert o coy manner that so often takes its place. The technique is ther still, it is even more brilliant, but it is now completely at th service of the role.

– Arnold Haskell – *London Musical Events,* April 195

THE 'BALLERINA TYPE'

Dame Ninette de Valois

An embryo ballerina has to have a very strange form of stamina which one cannot really label – it is outside the specific powers of strength that dancing demands. It is a special form of stamina that can 'live' through a whole evening, a very different thing from working in a short ballet where you hit a highlight for only a short time, perhaps for twenty minutes, but no more. The classic ballerina has to sustain a role for a matter of three hours. This depends very much on what we call the 'ballerina type'. Like Nerina, all the young dancers must have it if they are to become interpreters of the full-length ballets, and you can recognise it early on in them. You can find that a 'ballerina type' does not even come into her own until she has been given a full-length ballet; she may not be as successful in short works as other dancers who never become exponents of the long ballets; it is a completely different world. But you cannot produce the type; it is a quality within the dancer and is there from the very beginning.

Variations on a Theme: Ashton's ballet set to Benjamin Britten's 'Variations on a Theme of Purcell' was first staged on 6 January 1955 with designs by Peter Snow. **Below** David Blair, Nadia Nerina and Michael Boulton.

Alexander Grant, Rowena Jackson, Elaine Fifield and Nadia Nerina.

HOUSTON ROGERS

VARIATIONS ON A THEME

I remember that Elaine Fifield, Rowena Jackson and I had millions of steps – they nearly drove the three of us demented – 'knitting, tatting and crocheting' was what we called them. There was never more intricate, difficult choreography for three girls than those tiny complex steps. Whatever we did was terribly quick, complicated footwork – we were absolutely frantic with them. *NN*

In rehearsal.

BARRATT'S PHOTO PRESS

On 5 May 1956 the Sadler's Wells Ballet celebrated its 25th anniversary with a *pièce d'occasion* by Frederick Ashton, to music by Glazunov and with designs by André Levasseur. *Birthday Offering* featured the seven ballerinas of the company with their seven cavaliers: Michael Somes, Philip Chatfield, David Blair, Alexander Grant, Brian Ashbridge, Desmond Doyle and Brian Shaw.

From left to right: Svetlana Beriosova, Rowena Jackson, Elaine Fifield, Margot Fonteyn, Nadia Nerina, Violetta Elvin, Beryl Grey.

AURORA

The Sleeping Beauty *is the supreme achievement of nineteenth-century ballet. Staged in 1890 at the Maryinsky Theatre, St Petersburg,* Beauty *is the summation of everything its choreographer, Marius Petipa, worked for during his more than forty years service to the Imperial Ballet. It is a grand spectacular in which a glorious sequence of dances is gloriously set out to display the talents of a virtuoso ballerina and the technical resources of a great dance company. Inspired by Tchaikovsky's score, the seventy-one-year-old Petipa produced choreography of wonderful freshness and vivacity – could anything be more radiantly youthful than Aurora's first entrace and the succeeding Rose Adagio?*

When Ninette de Valois set about building a national ballet, one of her most significant actions was to acquire authentic stagings of the Imperial Russian classics as a necessary foundation for her company. Within three years (1932–4) Swan Lake, Casse Noisette, Giselle *and* Coppélia *were mounted at Sadler's Wells Theatre to provide a vital example and stimulus to dancers and audience. By 1939 the ensemble was strong enough to dance* Beauty*, and with the company's installation in its rightful home at Covent Garden in 1946, an opulent new production of* Beauty*, designed by Oliver Messel, announced to the world the maturity of our national ballet. Since then* The Sleeping Beauty *has become a 'signature' work for the Royal Ballet; with it the company triumphed on its first New York visit in 1949, and during the crucial visit to Russia in 1961 the company could take this greatest Russian ballet back to its birthplace with pride and assurance.* CC

Princess Aurora with the King, Derek Rencher, and the Queen, Gerd Larsen.

THE SLEEPING BEAUTY

Whenever I hear *The Sleeping Beauty* waltz in Act I nowadays, I still feel a chill. Aurora is one of the most difficult roles for a dancer – it is the ultimate in classicism. When I returned to dancing Aurora after working for a time on other parts, it was very taxing; it was like coming back to a corset, the very correct classical mould, with everything erect and upright.

I might have been dancing a series of *Filles*, or *Giselles*, and the thought of Aurora would delight me until there would be two or three really horrid rehearsals before I could get back into that classical corset. Once I felt it was all correct again, I could begin

to enjoy working on the role. It is absolutely essential to find the elegance and dignity that the *Beauty* steps demand; you have to be very pulled up and compact. *Giselle*, in this sense, is freer and more 'spread out', and *Fille* is just sheer happiness; but *Beauty* is so pure, so difficult in style, that it was really the greatest challenge. I always held it in the greatest awe; at first when I danced it, I still had technical problems, but later on the problems were those of the fineness of the steps, because there is a lot that is hidden in *Beauty*. It is not 'flashy', except perhaps in those big jumps of the first act solo; its difficulties lie in the little, tricky steps that may not look anything to an audience but which have to be done absolutely impeccably.

You have to come on stage in *Beauty* like a burst of sunshine, then launch almost straightaway into the Rose Adagio. It is the most difficult entrance in ballet – and as with *Swan Lake*, you have already been waiting for the whole of the first act, and have been in the theatre since five o'clock getting ready. I suppose it is a matter of concentration and discipline of mind. Sometimes I would be calm all day, and then take a deep breath as I went through the stage door (because you know you are not going to be allowed out until it is all over), and everything would be calm and under control as I sat down to make up. Then I would get on stage and simply freeze inside. It would be a matter of concentrating to make myself relax and get the feeling back into my feet and hands, because they would be like ice! On other days I might have been nervous all day, despite resting quietly before the performance; I would hardly be able to get my make-up on – eyebrows everywhere but the right place – then I would smell the theatre, and suddenly I would be quite calm and begin to enjoy being there. I could never bear to watch anyone dancing before I went on stage myself – my reaction was always that it was amazing how they could manage to dance, and even more amazing that I was proposing to do so. Only with *Beauty* would I go and watch the dancers in the Act I waltz to prepare myself emotionally for my entrance and try out a few balances holding on to a bit of scenery. Then ... you are on, and you start dancing straightaway. There is a brief moment of repose with the King and Queen – and then into the Rose Adagio! There you must have confidence in your four partners: the balances are difficult even for an experienced dancer and you must trust the boys; each one of you has to find an inner calm and concentration. The first set of balances are always more difficult than the second, because with the second series you are warmer, the first ones are over, and you hope that you have got the audience with you. Hands have to be in just the right position; the boys must not come forward too soon – or too late; they must not hold their hands out to you like a plate, because you want to take your time with the balances. If this second series goes well you feel marvellous when you take your bow to the audience. And if they go badly you want to go back and do them all over again – better. After the Adagio there is a solo, another entry, and then the dramatics of the spindle scene and the *danse de vertige*; and although the vision scene may seem lyrical and softer, you are dancing all the time. During the awakening, Petipa *forces* you to relax, because you are supposedly asleep on the bed; that is welcome because it gives a moment of utter repose to prepare yourself for the last act when you have to be brilliant and regal!

It was in *Beauty*, later on in my career, that something extraordinary happened during the last act solo. I was doing little steps across the stage, when I suddenly felt as if I were dancing in a bubble, and the whole audience was 'with' me – I felt as if everyone in the theatre was thinking of nothing but those sixteen little steps. It was a moment of utter magic, quite timeless; I was not conscious of doing anything technically, but afterwards, backstage, people said that something unique had happened. I have seen it and experienced it in the straight theatre, when you forget everything and are totally *with* the performer. There is no way of finding out what it is, and it comes very, very rarely: it happened with *Fille*, only for a moment, but it is the most exciting experience that can be found on stage, and is unforgettable. *NN*

Revival of *The Sleeping Beauty*, June 1960. Oliver Messel inspecting Aurora's costume during the dress parade in the Crush Bar of the Royal Opera House, Covent Garden.

EXIT

No dancer in this country, or, for that matter, in western Europe, has a classical technique to equal hers. It is a complete technique; she has speed and balance (to a remarkable degree) and she can jump; her timing is never at fault; and if her arm movements are made to appear no more than satisfactory (in a company blessed with dancers whose beauty of arm movement is outstanding), her precision and neatness of footwork are unrivalled in the Royal Ballet. Her line is almost always impeccable, and with all that, she has acquired that elegance of style which is even more necessary than her own natural gift of speed for a complete interpretation of Aurora's role in The Sleeping Beauty.

The Guardian, 9 January 1959

Dame Ninette de Valois

If we had not staged the classics right at the beginning – and I insisted upon that – I do not think that the choreographers and dancers would have achieved what they have. There had to be the classics – not just to see occasionally – it was necessary to be in close contact with them, both in their weaknesses and their strengths. And that was why Sergueyey was asked to reproduce them at Sadler's Wells with the original choreography, as far as was possible with our small company at that time.

The classics can always be expanded because their structure and form is so good, and I cut them as little as was possible. I used to overcrowd the stage in my effort to preserve the figurations, since you cannot cut the numbers of dancers in the big ensembles without ruining them – so the Sadler's Wells stage was sometimes awfully cramped! However I did not think that mattered because what we were trying to do was to preserve the whole, before it was lost.

HOUSTON ROGERS

The Rose Adagio with Desmond Doyle and Keith Rosson.

John Martin

Miss Nerina is completely adorable. She is pretty as a picture, has great charm, and can dance like a million dollars. Her body is beautifully placed, giving her lovely free arms and an unusually articulated torso. There are simply no problems of movement for her, and never so much as a hint of an ugly one. When Miss Nerina has developed a musical phrase to equal her command of the physical medium we shall all be fighting to drink champagne out of her slippers.

– *New York Times*, 23 September 1953

With the last act pas de deux there is nothing to distract you from the music and the steps, no characterisation to bother about. It is not just a question of the maturity of Aurora, but of the classic dance itself. There is nothing between the dancer and the dance, which is why, if you are going to produce classic dancers, you have to have *The Sleeping Beauty* in the repertoire. It is the epitome of classicism and it is therefore essential for the training of all classical dancers.

NN

The Act III pas de deux with David Blair.

BALLET ON TELEVISION

That television can popularise the arts is a commonplace; whether in popularising them it can do them justice is quite another matter. Of all the theatre arts, ballet is the most intractable for film and television treatment; the matters of space, of the large areas consumed by dancing, of the need to preserve the patterns and over-all shape of choreography, are fraught with difficulties for the film and television director. Too often in the cinema and on the small screen even the simplest duet is distorted and destroyed by close-ups or cleverly angled shots, a thing impossible on stage and quite alien to ballet. One answer has been found in the creation of special ballets for films and television, but there yet exists an implicit challenge for both media to try and show existing works by major companies and thereby to give an opportunity for the mass audience to enjoy an art which can often only properly be shown in a great metropolitan theatre.

It is one of the special merits of Margaret Dale's work for BBC television that, having been a distinguished dancer with the Royal Ballet, she is aware of the double – and sometimes conflicting – demands of choreography and camera. She has, in her many exceptional television presentations, developed a formula which permits ballets to be shown as honestly on the screen as in the theatre.

The benefits of television ballet are enormous, not least in the fostering of a new audience who may be encouraged to sample dancing in its proper home rather than at second hand. During the 1950s, Nadia Nerina and Alexis Rassine made regular television appearances; they reached an entirely new public during a series of monthly performances and when they made their concert tours throughout Britain, packed houses indicated how eager the public was to see dancers whom they had only known previously on television. CC

ANTHONY CRICKMAY

Margaret Dale with Keith Rosson as the Moor and Nadia Nerina as the Ballerina in *Petrushka* for BBC television.

PRODUCING BALLET FOR TELEVISION

Margaret Dale

Nadia Nerina, in 1957, was the only ballerina I knew who was prepared to take television seriously. It was a time when the great majority of people were apt to dismiss ballet on television as artistically inferior to the real thing; and the real thing, of course, was in the theatre. Certainly, it was true that many of the world's established ballet stars felt uncomfortable in a television studio. Everything was different, they missed the atmosphere – that warm contact with the audience – and most of all they missed their applause. When at the end of the performance there was no sound they felt flat and depressed; the silence left them feeling uncertain about their performance, they could not gauge how well or how badly they had done. So the whole thing was unsatisfactory to them. Somehow Nadia managed to overcome this. She accepted quite simply and without fuss that television was a different medium, that it had its own disciplines, and she was prepared to adapt herself to it. She managed to focus her thoughts on the unseen audience, she knew they numbered millions, and was aware that a huge percentage would be seeing her dance for the first time. Many were possibly also seeing ballet for the first time. So she was determined that she was going to give them absolutely nothing less than the real thing.

Between 1957 and 1965 Nadia played six important and difficult roles in six complete television ballet productions. All were serious, thoughtful studio adaptations of master works, consciously mounted for a mass audience. They were not recorded stage performances nor was it the intention to give the illusion of being at Covent Garden in a seat in the stalls; each ballet was minutely translated and re-worked for a different medium in the spirit of the original. They were:

1957 – 27 October	*Coppélia*
1958 – 6 April	*Les Sylphides*
1958 – 23 November	*Giselle*
1962 – 5 August	*Petrushka*
1962 – 27 December	*La Fille Mal Gardée*
1965 – 18 February	*The Firebird*

I think it could be said that had it not been for the 1958 *Giselle* we may not have seen the Royal Ballet productions that followed.

It all started in 1954 when I left the Royal Ballet and went to the BBC to do a television training course, though with no idea then of producing ballet for television. But in 1955 I was offered a year's contract as producer in the music department and though nothing was definitely stated I understood that my task was to put ballet of the highest possible standard on to the television screen. My first production was a ballet specially choreographed for television by a young Royal Ballet soloist, Kenneth MacMillan: its title, *Turned Out Proud.* To mount one ballet for television was a relatively easy matter; to do it on a regular basis, week after week or even month after month, was something else. BBC Television at the time simply was not geared to that sort of situation. To give but one example: there were no rehearsal rooms, nor even any suitable rooms in which to rehearse. A new ballet especially created for the screen could only be mounted very occasionally. Luckily at the same time there were many visiting companies coming to London – Pilar Lopez' Ballet Espagnol; Les Ballet Africains; the Moiseyev Ensemble, for instance. And it seemed to me to be quite a good idea for television to reflect, as it were, what was going on in London.

In that way I gained experience of shooting, lighting and cutting, and from the visiting companies I learned a lot about folk dance. It was a very happy time. Surprisingly, it was not difficult to persuade the visiting companies performing in London to give up their only free day, Sunday, to do a studio performance. Their managements thought of a television appearance as an extension of their visit to England and felt that it enabled them to be seen by a greater number of people. This was certainly the case in 1956 when the Bolshoy Ballet made their first visit to London. I went to see the Director, Mr Chulaki, and arranged to televise *Swan Lake* Act II, with Ulanova and Fadeyechev, at Riverside studios. During rehearsals I became quite friendly with Fadeyechev, despite the fact that we were unable to speak to each other. He did not speak English and I certainly did not speak Russian, but he understood all the little moves and changes that were necessary for the television cameras. He was helpful and intelligent, and I thought him charming as well as talented. Chulaki

Dr Coppélius, Robert Helpmann, bringing his Doll to life. BBC television production by Margaret Dale.

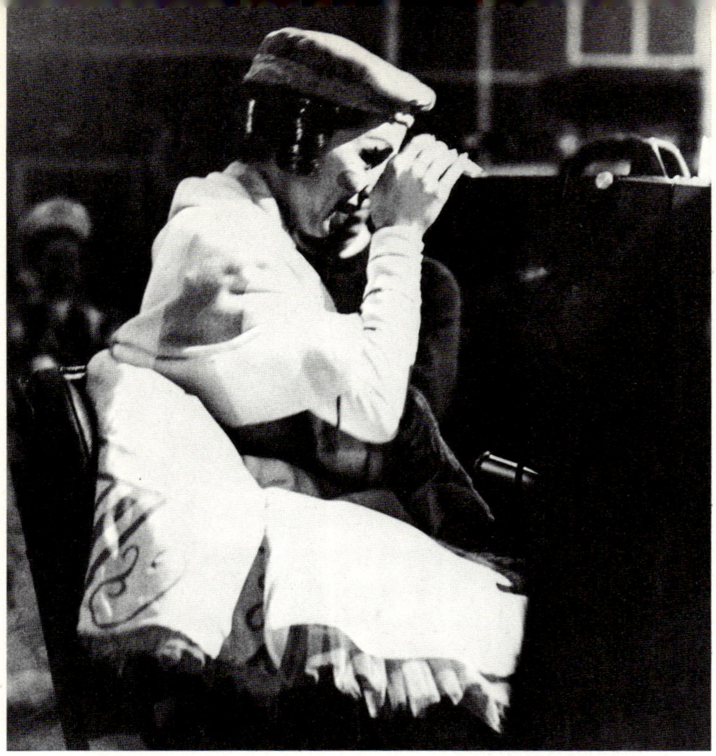

Petrushka: Keith Rosson as the Moor, Nadia Nerina as the Ballerina, Alexander Grant as Petrushka and Peter Franklin White as the Showman. In rehearsal at the BBC television studios.

also was very pleasant; cool and calm among all the bedlam there was at Covent Garden at the start of that season, and he agreed to this television performance during a very short meeting. He was a most straightforward man; if you asked a question he gave an immediate yes or no; there was no shilly-shallying and he also expected the same sort of directness in return. He appreciated that BBC Television was the major national network covering the country and thought that the Bolshoy Ballet had a duty to let the whole country see them.

After that transmission of *Swan Lake* Act II, quite apart from the popularity of the big Russian stars, Ulanova and Fadeyechev, it was obvious that the particular kind of ballet that the public wanted on television was classical. At the time it was impossible to persuade the established British ballet companies to spare the time to do productions for television. So I decided to attempt my own television production of the classics and not to do them 'faithfully' but 'unfaithfully', in the way I felt might make them really come alive on the television screen.

It was a big responsibility and it was essential to choose a ballet that I knew really well. I chose *Coppélia*, for the simple but practical reason that I could teach every role if necessary. Then, although I wanted the highest possible dancing standard, it was important to me that the plot was clear. With that thought in mind I asked Nadia, Robert Helpmann and Donald Britton to appear. They had all played the leading roles in *Coppélia* many

ANTHONY CRICKMAY

In Petrushka's cell. The Ballerina becomes frightened by Petrushka's advances.

times before and were delighted at the thought of giving their familiar old roles a slightly new interpretation.

Before rehearsals commenced, Nadia and I talked a lot about a different interpretation of Swanilda. I think she enjoyed this – at any rate we developed a good working relationship and came to trust each other. This TV *Coppélia* was successful, though it did not really surprise anybody; but what next? Television is relentless; before you finish one production you must be planning the next. And there are not that many classics that can be done. *Swan Lake* (in full) and *Sleeping Beauty* were too large in scale for television at that time; but there was *Giselle*. *Giselle* requires two big stars in the leading roles, but apart from that there are not many problems. Nadia had been dancing her first few performances of *Giselle* at Covent Garden, and I asked her if she thought she could do it for television, bearing in mind the fact that she would have to do both acts straight off, live, without an interval – most ballerinas would have been aghast at the suggestion. I thought it almost an impossibility – a physical and emotional marathon, and too much to ask. Nadia said she would think about it, and eventually said that she could. When she said that, I knew that she meant it and that we could rely on her. In the TV *Coppélia*, we had managed to give her a breathing space between Acts I and II by pre-filming her entering Dr Coppélius's house; this allowed her a two minute rest and also allowed us to move the scenery – if I remember correctly, Guy Shepherd had to design the ballet so that the interior set was hidden inside the exterior. Nothing could be flown in Riverside studios, because it was a low building. To get enough height was always a problem. In *Giselle* we found we were shooting off the top of the backcloth and into the lights. In those days it was quite unheard of to let the lights be seen! Shooting directly into light damaged the cathode tube, and cameramen were trained to ruin an artist's performance rather than shoot into the lights. But in *Giselle* during the big lifts in the second act, we broke that rule.

I have said that I thought it was a lot to ask a ballerina to do two acts of *Giselle* straight off; the reason it is so taxing is that after a long first act Giselle also has to recover from the emotionally exhausting 'mad' scene, then make a costume change and a complete change of mood for Act II. When Nadia said she could do it

Les Sylphides produced by Margaret Dale: the Mazurka with Philip Chatfield.

ANTHONY CRICKMAY

The Firebird on BBC television, directed by Patricia Foy.

she was also guaranteeing that she could rehearse it properly for the cameras – we had no understudy – yet without risk of accident. Studio floors are concrete, firm and rigid, otherwise the cameras would wobble, and it is always difficult to do any big role on a concrete floor, for it puts an undue strain on the tendons and calf-muscles.

Next: who was to play Albrecht? I had told Nadia that I would try to find a really internationally famous Albrecht. I made no promises, she left it to me, and I did not contact her for a long time, because I was wondering how one got a Russian dancer over to England for a television performance. I thought there would be endless problems, and in the end, as I did not know what to do, I thought I would just ask. So I picked up the telephone and phoned Mr Chulaki in Moscow. 'How do you feel', I said, 'about lending us a leading dancer to star in a BBC television production?' I knew that he had been quite pleased with the performance of *Swan Lake* that we had done the year previously. 'In principle,' he said 'no difficulties. Which dancer would you like to invite?' 'Fadeyechev', I said. Some months later, I went to the Brussels International Exhibition, and the Bolshoy Ballet were appearing at the Théâtre de la Monnaie. I saw Mr Chulaki again. This time there were no interpreters, so we spoke in rather basic French. Neither of us could manage small talk in French so the whole thing was over in about fifteen minutes – we stuck to the point. He said 'When, with whom, how much?' I said 'November, Nadia Nerina, £100 plus all expenses.' He smiled – it was done – and I came home and said to Nadia, 'I think I've got Fadeyechev for you, but keep it quiet.' I knew things could go wrong, but did not have anyone standing by as a second cast! I was beginning to get quite carried away with my success on the telephone, and rang around inviting other distinguished artists to appear in the supporting roles: Lydia Sokolova, Niels Bjorn Larsen, Alfred Rodrigues, Julia Farron. The ensemble was collected fairly quickly; a number of the girls had been in the previous *Coppélia*, and wanted to be in *Giselle*.

We were beginning to develop into a team; we worked hard in a Hammersmith rehearsal room for a week, fitting the production into the same floor space as we would have in Riverside studios.

ZOE DOMINIC

Giselle produced and directed for BBC television by Margaret Dale.

Above and right Mad scene: *Giselle* Act 1: Julia Farron as Bathilde, Alfred Rodrigues as the Duke of Courland, Nadia Nerina as Giselle and Nikolay Fadeyechev as Albrecht.

Above and below Lydia Sokolova as Berthe with Giselle.

ZOE DOMINIC

ZOE DOMINIC

Giselle's solo Act 1.

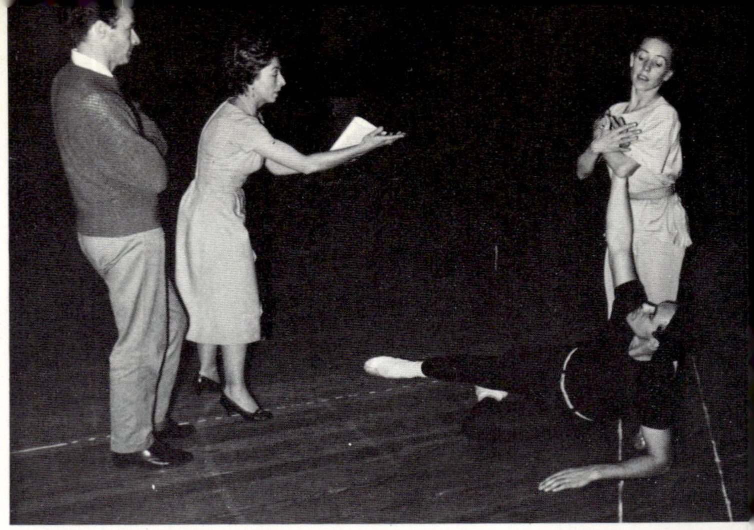

In rehearsal: Margaret Dale, Peter Wright, Nadia Nerina and Nikolay Fadeyechev.

Death of Giselle: Nerina, Fadeyechev, Sokolova and Niels Bjorn Larsen as Hilarion.

ZOE DOMINIC

A pause in rehearsal: Margaret Dale, Nerina and Fadeyechev.

Fadeyechev as Albrecht

Nerina and Fadeyechev – *Giselle* Act II.

It was necessary to change the timing of some small actions, usually by about a bar. On stage two important moments can happen simultaneously and the eye can take it all in, but in television one often requires a separate shot for each action, so each must be treated separately and minor adjustments in musical phrasing have to be rehearsed: this is the sort of thing that takes the time at rehearsal. Fadeyechev was due to arrive on the Monday morning of the second week, and Nadia and I went to the airport to meet him. After being taken to his hotel, he just checked in, unpacked his practice clothes, and came with us straight to rehearsal. When we walked into the rehearsal room with him, the whole corps de ballet gasped. Hardly a word was spoken. I simply asked him where he wanted to start; he said 'Act II', and Nadia and he went straight into the Act II pas de deux and immediately danced as if they had been working together for years. He was completely in charge. Nadia was very pliable, very willing, easy. They were marvellous together. They never once phrased things differently, lifts and catches all worked. From then on the whole production went swingingly, with a real sense of excitement.

We had some production problems with the scale of the setting, but luckily the quality of the performance was so fine that it was hardly noticed. As I have said, the studio was very low, of course, and we were transmitting the ballet live. The first act set was struck and rolled away on castors as soon as the act ended – while Act II started in the adjacent smaller studio. Albrecht had to change on the spot. (I seem to remember that he changed inside his 'house', there was not even time for him to get to the dressing room.) I treated the first act like a drama, but the second act is pure dance and there were moments in that production when Nadia and Fadeyechev danced so beautifully, it was quite sublime. By the time the Act II pas de deux began, we in the studio were not caring if the lights showed – the performance took over.

ZOE DOMINIC

Giselle and Albrecht with the Queen of the Wilis, danced by Margaret Hill.

AWAY FROM THE ROYAL OPERA HOUSE

More than any other dancer of her generation, Nadia Nerina ventured beyond the confines of the Opera House to dance for a larger public. In 1952 she went to South Africa with Alexis Rassine, in a concert tour that culminated in a series of performances of the full-length Swan Lake *in Johannesburg with the local ballet society.*

She returned to South Africa in 1954 for the Durban Centenary celebrations, and in the following year toured with Alexis Rassine for 35,000 miles in South Africa, Rhodesia, East and West Africa, finishing with a fortnight's series of performances of Giselle *with Dulcie Howes' Cape Town Ballet Club.*

From these concert performances there came the idea of touring the British Isles during 1956–7 with Alexis Rassine and the pianists Colin Kingsley and Cyril Preedy. 1958 brought a six-week season at the Palace Theatre, London, in a variety bill which included Frankie Vaughan, Hetty King, Bernard Miles and Petula Clark – with Nadia Nerina dancing the Dying Swan and the Act III Swan Lake *duet (partnered by Veit Bethke) twice nightly in a theatre where, forty-eight years before, Pavlova had danced the Dying Swan in a variety bill.*

Nadia Nerina and David Blair also gave concert performances at the Royal Albert Hall and the Royal Festival Hall as part of orchestral programmes in 1958, 1959 and 1960. As with many ballerinas, Nerina made extensive appearances throughout the world – visits to Germany, Turkey, Finland, Denmark and the United States were a recurrent feature in her career, as guest with major companies.

In addition, two roles were created for her away from the Royal Ballet: as the Girl in Western Theatre Ballet's Home *and the warrior heroine Clorinda in Monteverdi's* Combattimento di Tancredi e Clorinda *at the Aldeburgh Festival.* CC

Cape Town 1955 – seven performances of *Giselle* in a week.

DANCING WITH NADIA

Alexis Rassine

I first met Nadia when she had just arrived in London from South Africa, and was a stand-on in the Prologue of *The Sleeping Beauty* at Covent Garden. I remember noticing her work in class. There was something spring-like about her, a terrific *joie de vivre*, a vitality in her dancing which made it obvious that she would 'go somewhere'. I remember, too, that in class she showed even then a very strong technique, and when I came to partner her for the first time in *Les Sylphides*, she was very easy to work with – one of the easiest ballerinas I ever had to partner. There was never any difficulty in lifting her because she had great *ballon* and spring, unlike some ballerinas, with whom lifts can be hard work.

Nadia was the most 'Russian' of dancers that this country has

HOUSTON ROGERS

With Alexis Rassine in *L'Après-Midi d'un Faune* and in *La Cachucha* choreographed by Elsa Brunelleschi.

produced: when Konstantin Sergueyev was last in London with the Kirov Ballet, he asked me to help him revive *L'Après-Midi d'un Faune* for the Kirov because it was a role I knew; and he said to me then, 'It is hard to realise that Nerina is English: she dances more like a Russian girl.'

The average English dancer tends to look very neat, clean, detached; with Nerina there was an attack and a brilliance – a bite to her dancing. I do not think that our ballet has ever produced a dancer of such virtuosity; Nerina's elevation could be the envy of many a premier danseur. She was one of the few artists who was a truly magical Firebird because she could encompass those fantastic jumps across the stage.

I worked with her in *Les Sylphides, Coppélia, Giselle, Sylvia, Swan Lake* and *Beauty*. When I taught her the role of Giselle in South Africa for our guest performances, I liked her dedicated approach to work; she was one of those exceptional dancers prepared to go on and on working. Some artists will go once through a scene fully and thereafter will 'mark' in rehearsal – just indicating steps – to save their strength. Nadia would always work full-out in rehearsals, which was one of the things I loved especially about her. We danced together instinctively; we were alike in physique and we had an instant muscular rapport which meant we worked without problems. One thing always stands out in my mind: Nadia's tremendous confidence once she went on stage. She might be nervous at rehearsal, but when the curtain rose she was as cool as a cucumber. If a dancer is nervous, it can be infectious – one ballerina I remember was always very edgy in the Bluebird pas de deux, and that was dangerously catching. But Nerina was always assured on stage, and that is very rare.

We did a whole year of television appearances which gave us a public for our touring performances, when we would appear in theatres that usually took a whole ballet company. We danced six performances a week – and I cannot remember another ballerina able to sustain the demands of all the point work.

THE DRAGONFLY

Pavlova's choreography for *Dragonfly* was taught me by Cleo Nordi. She thought I was the only other dancer to have performed it since Pavlova died. It has masses of little pas de bourrée, very simple and very, very fast in fifth position, and a great many grands jetés, forward and turning. It never stops except for the few seconds when the dragonfly alights on the ground and plays with its wings – you have only a couple of seconds to catch your breath before you are darting off again. It was the most tiring solo, apart from *Firebird*, that I have ever danced, and it lasts only a minute and a half! Like other Pavlova solos it looks deceptively easy. *NN*

We enjoyed dancing in this huge hall – the challenge of projecting ballet in a vast space was tremendously appealing. When we danced *Swan Lake*, under the stars in the enormous open-air Hollywood Bowl, the feeling of freedom was exhilarating. *NN*

HOUSTON ROGERS

On the Albert Hall stage, 1959. Black Swan pas de deux with David Blair.

'BALLET HIGHLIGHTS' CONCERT TOUR

Alexis Rassine and I arranged to give six concert performances weekly in four of the major provincial cities – Oxford, Leeds, Liverpool and Manchester. The concerts were to be similar in form to those we had danced on our extensive 'Ballet Highlights' concert tour throughout South Africa. The two-hour programme would consist of five pas de deux and between the dances the two concert pianists would play musical extracts, as well as accompanying our numbers.

We rehearsed every detail in London so that the programme would run easily with no undue pauses. After the opening night at the New Theatre in Oxford we were all celebrating with a glass of champagne in my dressing room when the theatre manager came up to me and said 'Can I have a word with you, Miss Nerina?' He told me he was 'awfully worried about the performance'. I was puzzled; the applause had seemed very warm and from what we could judge the audience had enjoyed themselves. The manager agreed, 'Oh yes, of course, tremendous value, a great show – but it only lasted an hour and a half!' We simply could not believe it – but amazingly enough, the curtain had come down just after 9.00 pm. No audience could have seen so much dancing, or so many costume changes, in so short a time. Then we realized what had happened. Everything had gone so smoothly, our stage manager had been so quick, and we had changed with such lightning speed that we had clipped half an hour off the running time. Next night, with the same programme, we all relaxed, and the missing half hour was back. *NN*

WORKING TOGETHER

David Blair

We worked very well together, and I loved partnering Nerina because she had no fear. One could take enormous risks with her, and it was always my idea of pleasure to show her off as best I could and give her plenty of space. She would attack an arabesque as if I were not there, and I would always catch her at the last moment; she trusted me completely. We were also aware that in the solos we were in competition, though always of the friendliest kind. If I did double tours in Black Swan, then Nadia would have to cap that in her solo; and in the coda after she had done thirty-two impeccable fouettés I would have to match that in grandes pirouettes. We found it very exciting, and I think we found each other at the right time in our careers.

FIRST GISELLE

I had seen Act II danced by the Rambert Company in 1945. This had been my first experience of seeing a professional company and I was unimpressed by the Wilis, particularly by the classical mime which appeared rather foolish to me. My lack of interest in this particular ballet lingered on for many years, but then something rather strange happened. I was in Boston on an American tour with our Company and feeling very unhappy. My first romance had gone terribly wrong, and one night I came back to my hotel room with my bouquet of flowers from the performance. I was still upset and started to throw the flowers about the room. Suddenly I caught sight of myself in the mirror, and for some reason, a memory of Giselle's mad-scene flashed through my mind. When I woke up the next morning the flowers were still littered around the room. My behaviour seemed ridiculous, but something about the mad scene in *Giselle* remained with me. Over the next few months I became conscious that this experience had awakened the desire to dance the role and the opportunity to do this arose when Alexis Rassine and I were returning for our second long concert tour of South Africa in 1955. We had been invited to dance a three-week season of the full production of *Giselle*, supported by the Cape Town ballet company.

Alexis Rassine was our Company's leading Albrecht; he had danced with all the company ballerinas, and he coached me for the role. What I had to learn for myself was how to interpret it and at first I thought I had to 'live' the first act and believe in it so intensely that the drama would come over to the audience. I got very emotional, recalling the Boston incident, trying to relive that experience honestly for the performance. The result was that by the end of the first act I was completely worn out and in floods of tears, with the mascara pouring down my face and hardly calm enough to get ready for Act II. After several performances like this – and we had to dance eighteen in three weeks – I thought this was certainly not the way to go mad on stage! I learned, there and then, an invaluable lesson. One must use all experience but it must be controlled. At first I thought this was not honest but I gradually appreciated that although one might understand an emotion it had to be given theatrical shape – not presented in the raw.

Before I danced Giselle at Covent Garden, Dame Ninette, who had recently returned from a visit to Moscow, told me in rehearsal how in the Stanislavsky production Giselle rushed to the back of the stage after she had lost her reason, just as if she was fleeing to the end of the world to escape her fear. I tried the run and the effect was electric. It felt instantly true within my concept of the mood at that particular moment: to create a character one has to find something within oneself, something true, which will sustain the role.

NN

Rehearsing in South Africa with Alexis Rassine.

A.R. TANNER

CIRCUS AND CLOWNS

I was told I was going to dance in a circus, which seemed quite extraordinary, with Sir Adrian Boult conducting, and with choreography by Alan Carter. We went to Olympia, twelve boys from the company and myself, and they put down flooring on the ring. I can just remember that I had to balance on a small stool turning round and round, and the boys eventually carried me off. The clowns seemed fascinated by us; I think they realized that we were professionals and worked very hard, because after the performance they shook hands with each of us, accepting us as part of the Big Top. *NN*

Nadia Nerina with dancers from the Sadler's Wells Theatre Ballet.
On 18 December 1952 the Variety Club of Great Britain presented a Royal Performance of Bertram Mills Circus before the Queen and Prince Philip. The surprise of the evening was a ballet created by Alan Carter, to part of Suppé's *Poet and Peasant* overture conducted by Sir Adrian Boult.

THE DYING SWAN

Every aspiring dancer thinks about the Pavlova swan. I was going to private classes with Cleo Nordi, who had danced with Pavlova, and one day she said she would like to teach me the Dying Swan. She taught with great dedication because she had been in the Pavlova Company for many years and had watched Pavlova dance it night after night from the wings. There is a published illustrated version of the dance which Anatol Chujoy, the late dance historian, showed me in America. This is much more complicated because it was the version that Fokine originally choreographed for his wife. But Madame Nordi showed me the version as Pavlova danced it, which, over the years, she had simplified, paring away most of the steps to leave only those movements which were essential for the interpretation. Madame Nordi was particularly illuminating about the arm movements. Because Fokine had been interested in Isadora Duncan's style of free movement, these are not the 'classical' *Swan Lake* arms, but rounder, and they move continuously from the centre of the back, with the palms of the hands upwards. The result is an image of a swan that is softer and more emotional. The essence of this poetic solo is not of a bird dying but the freeing of a soul. *NN*

ANTHONY CRICKMAY

Left Nadia Narina as the schizophrenic Girl, Simon Mottram as the Doctor and Leo Guerard as the Boy. **Right** Peter Darrell, the choreographer of *Home*, with designer Peter Cazalet.

THE CREATION OF *HOME*

Peter Darrell, *Director of The Scottish Ballet*

At the time I staged *Home* I was very interested in making ballets with playwrights, and John Mortimer came up with an idea which I liked. I think now that the libretto was perhaps too personal to Mortimer for it to work for me as well, and I was never completely satisfied with the way the ballet ended.

The Western Theatre Ballet had been invited to appear at the Sunderland Festival with a star name, and because I had known Nadia for a long time, I asked her to dance with us. I found her very responsive and rewarding to work with – she had done all her 'homework' before we started work: she knew the Bartok score before rehearsals began – and I made the role of the girl very individually hers. Nadia was very expressive through her technique; her body was highly responsive, and her instinct for movement meant that it was an 'intelligent' body. If she had been more overtly emotional in her dancing, this would have pushed the role too far; Nadia had a 'withheld' quality that was right for the girl. With a different dancer the role could have become a wallow, but Nadia kept it within bounds: I found her very moving, and her technical command, which I remembered from when we were in *Mardi Gras* together, was amazing. I do not think that I exploited Nadia's technique, but I did use it differently. The role of the girl was the best written in the ballet, and I think that the family came across quite well: they were understood by Mortimer and me. But I do not feel that the inmates of the mental home came across quite as well, though John Mortimer gave me a little story-line on each one. Perhaps I should have done more research into people in that sort of home, because I never felt I 'knew' them as I 'knew' the girl's family.

Clement Crisp

Sunderland's North-Eastern Theatre Festival is a bright enterprise, all the brighter for asking Western Theatre Ballet to participate and to feature Nadia Nerina as a guest in a dramatic role specially created for her. The resultant Home *is a good work, with flaws; it is certainly not just a vehicle for a guest ballerina, but a valid extension of WTB's policy of offering sharply contemporary dance-pieces.*

The theme, devised by John Mortimer, tells of a sad, ugly-duckling of a girl, emotionally unstable, doomed to grow into an ugly duck, who is packed off to a mental home by her grey, uncomprehending family. This shock plunges the girl deeper into neurosis, but she finds ultimately a companionship and sympathy she has never previously known among her fellow-inmates – even a fragile love relationship with one of them. She rejects her family irrevocably: as you can see, all that is missing from the title are the words 'is where the heart is'.

Peter Darrell, the choreographer, has been set a difficult task by the music – Bartok's fifth quartet – and more especially by the scenario, which lacks tension in its dramatic development. The first half of the ballet, up to the girl's committal, is urgent, heart-touching; Darrell's difficulty has been to reconcile the diffuse elements in the second half – the interaction of the other patients with the girl and her family – and the music. Nevertheless, the work does succeed, commenting succinctly on the emotional needs of its characters, and using a dance language that makes interesting use of formal dance movement and naturalistic gesture.

Perhaps the most fascinating aspect of Nerina's performance is not the sympathy and delicacy of her portrayal of the girl, though these are admirable, but the fact that she never for an instant appears to be a guest artist. She assumes the company's dramatic style, which is distinguished by its maturity – and is absorbed into a team of remarkably expressive artists. Of course her dancing is fine: her technical ease will always be a joy to watch, but in her tense quick steps, in the sharply anguished outlines that Darrell has devised and which make such good use of her powers, it is the pathetic creature who is presented and not the ballerina.

Nerina and Darrell give us a study in bewildered unhappiness; the girl's frantic eagerness to please her family, the clumsy failure of her every attempt at normality, are all sensitively shown; packed off to the institution with a hideous flowered hat plonked on her head, Nerina makes an unforgettably moving figure of the girl. All her effects are closely controlled by a sense of unyielding desolation, with only one frantic outburst when she realises she is trapped in the institution. In short, it is an unusual and worthwhile creation. There are good, imaginative designs by Peter Cazelet, and equally good and imaginative playing from WTB's artists.

– *The Financial Times,* 8 February 1965

ANTHONY CRICKMAY

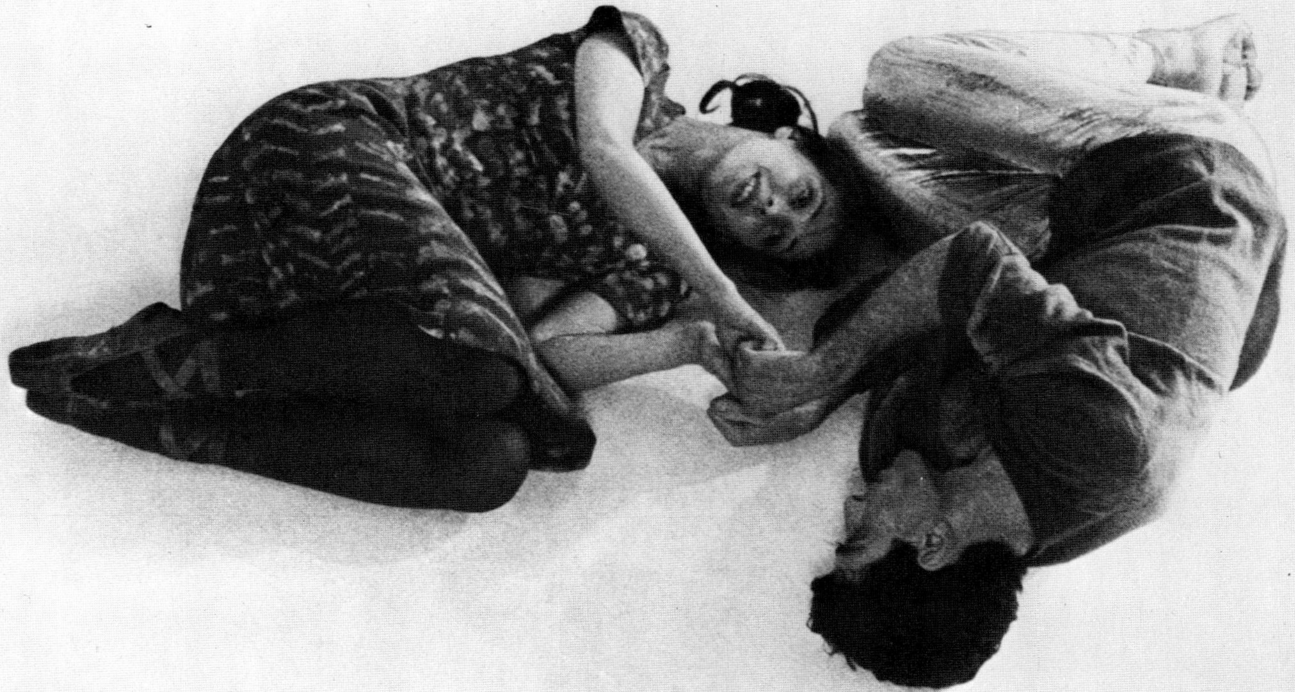

The final moment of *Home*.

Il Combattimento di Tancredi e Clorinda *was first performed at The Maltings, Snape, on 23 June 1967, in celebration of the quatercentenary of Monteverdi's birth. The production was by Leo Kersley, with choreography by Janet Sinclair. Tancredi was sung by John Carol Case and danced by Leo Kersley; Clorinda was sung by April Cantelo and danced by Nadia Nerina; the Narrator was Peter Pears.*

TANCREDI AT ALDEBURGH

Leo Kersley

It was Nadia's work in *Il Combattimento di Tancredi e Clorinda*, which must have been among her last – if not *the* last – created roles, which confirmed my long-held conviction that she was the most versatile of all British ballerinas. Fokine, Massine, Ashton, Howard, de Valois, Balanchine – she could dance all of them without strain and convince her audience as Aurora, Odette/Odile, Swanilda, Lise, Ondine, Giselle, the Firebird, Mam'zelle Angot, Columbine, Elektra and many more. Possibly her most notable facility was for taking over a role from a dramatic dancer – June Brae in *The Vagabonds*, Sheilah O'Reilly in *Khadra* – and making it equally convincing by dancing as opposed to acting it.

What came out in all these roles, and was able to come out so strongly because her technique was so flawless that it did not impair or hinder her interpretation, was the completeness of a rounded, mature human being who had made her way to the top through her own efforts and been spared very few sorrows and sufferings on the way. It is the loss of this complete personality, added to the perfectly tuned and trained instrument, which makes me very sad that Nadia's dancing does not exist any more except in the memories of those fortunate enough to have seen her on the stage, or – more fortunate still – to have danced with her.

Tancredi at the Maltings with Leo Kersley.

LA FILLE MAL GARDEE

Sunny, joyous Fille *took the stage of the Royal Opera House, Covent Garden, on 28 January 1960, won our hearts totally and then has never let them go. Few ballets have known such instantaneous success, nor merited it so richly. Few ballets have better demonstrated that mysterious exchange between a choreographer and his dancers in which mutual inspiration begets delight upon delight without seeming either forced or artificial. In performance today, as when it was first written,* Fille *generates a happiness that is almost tangible; it was a ballet written with delight in its original interpreters, and that quality still shines in every Royal Ballet presentation. It remains a most searching and happy portrait of a particular epoch in the Royal Ballet's history: its first cast were all virtuosi in their various styles, from the comic genius of Alexander Grant and Stanley Holden and the joviality of Leslie Edwards, to the brilliance and charm of David Blair and Nadia Nerina's adorable ebullience and that special radiance that she gave to even the most ferocious technical feats. After more than a decade the ballet has known dozens of fine interpreters – testimony to the quality of the Royal Ballet's dancers and to the example offered by the original cast – but to those of us fortunate enough to have seen the first performances nothing can ever eclipse their magic: they were the stuff that legends are made of.* CC

La Fille Mal Gardée was given its first performance by the Royal Ballet at the Royal Opera House, Covent Garden, on Thursday 28 January 1960, with choreography by Frederick Ashton, scenery and costumes by Osbert Lancaster, music by Ferdinand Hérold – freely adapted and arranged from the 1828 version by John Lanchbery – and conducted by Hugo Rignold. The ballet's success on the first night was absolute, as it has been ever since. The cast included: Nadia Nerina as Lise; David Blair as Colas; Alexander Grant as Alain; Stanley Holden as Widow Simone; Leslie Edwards as Thomas.

ZOE DOMINIC

Frederick Ashton rehearsing Nerina and Blair.

ZOE DOMINIC

THE IDEAL CAST

Sir Frederick Ashton

My cast is ideal. All are true, all became real before my eyes. They danced themselves into their roles. It was a pleasure to feel their joy as the ballet unfolded itself to its end. But do not let us forget Dauberval: his is the masterly balletic conception, his characters are rounded and his action carries through to the end. The piece displays the most lively *sens du théâtre* in the clever arrangement of effective situations and charming tableaux. The interest is kept up to the end: at the very last moment I added the reappearance of Alain as a final coup. The popularity of the ballet is certainly not due to any originality in the subject but rather that it lends itself to be infused with new life. I wanted to re-exploit the fun in my characters, to give the ballet a frank, open gaiety combined with an effortless lyricism and to develop the theme of ribbons as a kind of leitmotif, or as themes are developed in a symphony. Our success astounded me. I have given more of myself to other ballets with less result. The next day the cocks crowed in jubilation, passing the good news from one to the other throughout the countryside. Oh, what a heavenly morning.

ZOE DOMINIC

Top of page Ashton, Stanley Holden, Nadia Nerina, Alexander Grant and David Blair.
Above Ashton rehearsing the pas de trois Act I – Colas, Lise and Alain.

HOUSTON ROGERS

Lise and Colas.

Mary Clarke

Nerina plays the mime scenes with enchanting ease and confidence and humour; she dances throughout like an angel, and I was reminded of the phrase used by the nineteenth-century Russian critic Gribiyedov about the ballerina Teleshova: 'each of her leaps is like a shower of stars'.

– *The Dancing Times,* March 1960

Clive Barnes

The ballet's triumph is to be found simply in Ashton's choreography and – for even a Stradivarius needs a fiddler – the truly astonishing virtuosity of its cast. He has taken Nadia Nerina and David Blair, the two most spectacular dancers in British ballet, and made them dance as they have never danced before. Ashton works on his dancers rather like a sculptor, quarrying and carving his choreography out of their very bodies ... and has started afresh with Nerina and Blair in a new vein of bravura choreography.

... These two fly high above the stage, twisting and turning like aerobatic birds. Blair, aggressively confident and defiantly elegant, turns round with the cutting force of steel, and when it comes to partnering he holds Nerina right above his head in ecstatic Bolshoy lifts. Nerina is fast and dazzling; she jumps and curvets around the stage with the athletic power of a man, yet with a completely feminine flounce, madcap and girlish.

– *The Spectator,* 5 February 1960

Clement Crisp

The magnificence of the choreography apart, Fille *is extraordinary for the dancing of its principals. Absolute authority in any form of interpretive art is so rare that to find it in the four leads in one ballet makes for outstanding theatrical pleasure. Nerina's Lise is one of the company's treasures; at times her dancing resembles great coloratura, with the roulades and decorations of the choreographic line pearling out with fantastic ease (so that we might well call her La Stupenda), while the freedom and lightness of her jumps and beats, the brilliance of accent and clarity of line give unalloyed pleasure. At the most dazzling moments, when it seems impossible that she can jump higher or hold an attitude longer, a smile will flash out to let us know that she is sharing our enjoyment. It is glorious dancing and as exciting as anything we have seen this summer.*

– *The Financial Times,* 18 September 1963

THE CREATION OF *FILLE*

David Blair

By the time we came to work on *Fille*, Nadia and I had established a partnership over a long period – we had first danced together in *Coppélia* in 1954 – and to me she was always a tremendous challenge. There had grown up between us a professional relationship which was rather like 'anything you can do, I can do better', and I think that this was a kind of challenge to Ashton too. He came to the *Fille* rehearsals with a typed scenario, so that we all knew exactly what the action was going to be. He also had a very clear idea of the framework, where all the lifts were, the cat's cradle, for instance, and the pas de deux. I think a lot of the steps, though, were a result of the abrasion he set up between Nadia and me, by encouraging us to compete against each other.

ANTHONY CRICKMAY

The only other ballet I recall which seemed to write itself quite so easily, with never a step rubbed out, was *Pineapple Poll*. *Fille* is so well constructed that the steps came naturally, in the sense that Ashton cajoled us to do more and more during rehearsals. If we did a single step, he would say 'Can't you do a double?', and he was continuously urging us to reach our limits. When we came to the Fanny Elssler pas de deux, he did not seem to know quite how he wanted to end it, though he knew he wanted to finish with a big climax. We had never run through everything he had written until then, but he said he would like a stunning finale. Nadia and I had been practising for hours all sorts of one-handed lifts, with me running round the studio and Nadia high in the air, and when we did one for him, Ashton said 'That's it'.

But then, when we tried to put it all together, we realised the sort of obstacle race we had set ourselves. Nevertheless, we felt strong enough to carry it off. I remember that one night Ashton took us to see the Georgian dancers at the Albert Hall, where the men danced on points doing very fast steps, and that is what inspired the fast little steps in Nadia's solo. Ashton is a marvellous selector, and his genius picks out and moulds all the material he finds to make great choreography.

Dancers sometimes think that they themselves have written part of a ballet with Ashton, but in fact he always comes well prepared to rehearsals. He may not have the exact steps planned, but the construction is crystal clear in his mind.

Fille was pure joy to work on, and Nadia was pure joy to work with. The mime scene in Act II was written very, very fast, three days after my twin daughters were born. I went to see my wife, Maryon Lane, in hospital, and then rushed to Drury Lane where Nadia and I were dancing the *Don Quixote* pas de deux at a charity gala, and then, because of rehearsal schedules and because the choreography was flowing so well, we went to the Baron's Court studios to work with Ashton, tired as we were. The whole section, from the mime scene where Lise is left alone to the scene where Colas jumps out of the hay right up to the moment where he kisses her and they hear Simone returning, was done in half an hour. We started at 5.30 and were finished by 6.00. Sir Frederick had done his homework with Karsavina; he knew the mime scene and taught it to Nadia, who was very quick to learn, and we finished the whole thing amazingly quickly when you consider how tender and touching it is.

Fille was a lovely ballet on which to work, joyful in rehearsal, and seeming to flow right from the start – Ashton created it in six weeks. I shall never forget the first rehearsal when Sir Frederick said, 'Just do something – she's a pretty village girl.' The music is so lyrical and charming that it gave the feeling straight away. We had fun with the cat's cradle; Ashton showed us how to do it with our fingers and then we tried to do it with our bodies

and the ribbons. When I was being supported by all the ribbons held by the girls, they kept running round and I stayed up and turned too, and kept on turning. Ashton was thrilled. Incidents like that kept on happening, and working with Ashton was marvellous. He might say 'I want you looking like smoke in the air', so David Blair and I would do a lift, and Ashton's genius, working on us, transformed it into something glorious. *NN*

TEMPO RUBATO

Timing in passages of elevation has to catch the rhythmic nuance of the music; this not only helps one to jump but also highlights the steps of elevation. Lise's flying circuit round the stage in the coda of the corn-field duet in Act I takes the form of *chassé-coupé-chassé-jeté en tournant* – step-step-step-*grand jeté* – with landings on the musical beat. But when Lise comes to *battement devant en temps levé* followed by three *battements en cloche fouetté en temps levé* the beat comes as the working leg passes through first position and the accent falls on the *temps levé*, so that there will be an extra beat left at the end of the phrase, and this Lise should use to 'fill out' the final position in *arabesque en l'air*.

There is really a question of *tempo rubato* here; by the time Lise reaches that final arabesque she will in effect have 'gained' half a beat which should be used at the end of the phrase to hold and thus highlight the final arabesque. It is the joy of that final position which Lise feels, and which the dancer must show to the audience. Dancers will understand how important this is, and future Lises may even be interested to know how I phrased the steps. *NN*

Andrew Porter –

The ballet has been written for Nadia Nerina and David Blair, both virtuosos of the first order and at the same time classical interpreters of uncommon intelligence, sensibility and imagination. There is no one today who can dance like Nerina. During the last few seasons as her Aurora, Odette–Odile, *Giselle and Swanilda have grown ever more wonderful, we have longed for her to be given a role just such as this, which would draw upon her technique as extravagantly as the most spectacular concert number a Balanchine could devise, yet do it within the context of a consistent dramatic conception. ... For the first time Ashton has been able to compose without giving a thought to technical limitations. Like all great choreographers he is inspired by his dancers – and they by him. He has revealed facet after facet of Fonteyn's genius – and she of his. And now from Nerina and Blair he has received a quite different sort of inspiration; and written a ballet quite unlike any he has done before.*

The Financial Times, 29 January 1960

Richard Buckle

Nerina and Blair have never been so good before, or had such wonderful steps to do. Victor Hugo wrote 'Quand on est jeune, on a des matins triomphants', *and dancing of this kind, which is* perhaps *the highest kind, imparts the pang of wonder we had on summer mornings when we were young and ran to bathe with bare feet on the dew. His amazing corkscrew turns, her joyous écarté, their* pas de ruban *in which they wind each other spinning in and out before knotting themselves into a cat's cradle, his lifting her at one arm's length above him like a shining prize, her tripping runs, his great spins, their tenderness and gaiety together – these are a few memories from a triumphant evening.*

– *The Sunday Times*, 31 January 1960

LISE'S COSTUMES

The only shadow during the whole production, as far as I was concerned, was Osbert's original concept of the costumes for Lise. My costume was always crucial to my interpretation of any role, and extremely important to me. Originally Lise's dresses were stiff and in brilliant reds and greens. Osbert Lancaster had not seen what we were doing in rehearsal, and when I saw the Lise designs I burst into tears. I felt I could not interpret the character of Lise in these very sharp colours – she should wear pastel shades, soft blues and pinks. Osbert was understanding. When he asked me what I thought, I made a little sketch and he worked from that. I could not have danced the role in the original designs: I knew that to create Lise I had to wear dresses that were sympathetic to her character. *NN*

I regard *Fille* as one of Sir Frederick Ashton's major achievements. When we put it into the repertory, it was important because it represented a certain period of classic ballet which was lacking from our repertory; it was the sort of early classic ballet that did not really come back into fashion until *Coppélia* in 1870. It was a ballet that required a very special style of ballerina, and Nadia Nerina was ideally cast and had the biggest success of her career as Lise. One might say that it is a 'soubrette ballerina' role, but nevertheless the great ballerinas have danced it – Karsavina, Pavlova, and many more.

Dame Ninette de Valois

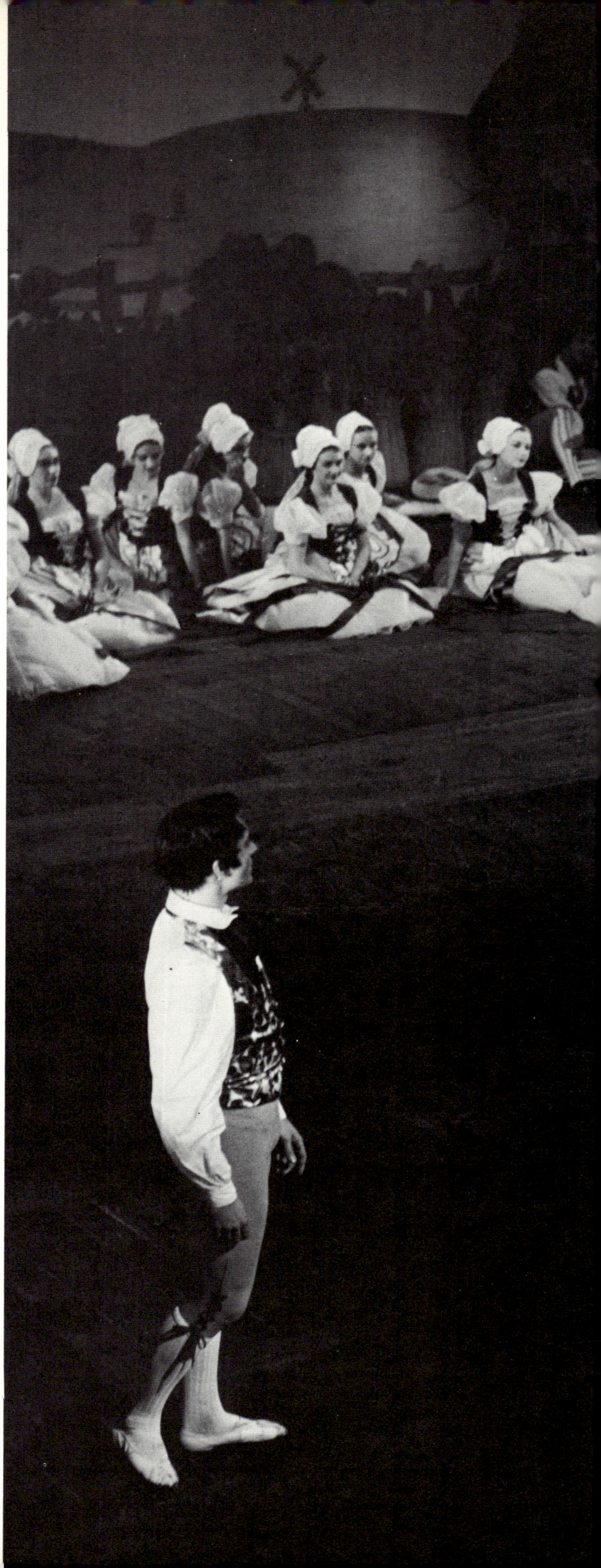

HOUSTON ROGERS

I always thought of Lise as a girl with a distinct personality. She is most endearing, with a delicious and inventive sense of humour; she is immensely fond of her mother, but slightly independent; she is young, and perhaps child-like, yet there is an innate maturity and good sense about her. In her famous mime-scene she dreams of the joy of having children and understands what marriage will mean. But her character is quite unlike Swanilda in *Coppélia*: she, too, has a sense of fun, but she is forward, mischievous, naughty, and although she has a brittle charm, she is heartless in her teasing of Dr Coppélius – she needs a good spanking. Lise is gentle in her fun, in a very feminine way. If you listen to the music for *Fille*, Lise's melodies are just like her: light, lyrical, warm, tender.

NN

HOUSTON ROGERS

Above left Lise teasing her mother.
Left Lise's mime scene in Act II.
Opposite Colas comforting Lise after the mime scene.

HOUSTON ROGERS

Above Lise and Colas imploring Simone to bless their marriage.
Right Lise and her friends: the finale.

The whole rehearsal period went with such happiness: like the ballet it seemed to flow from the very beginning. Everything follows on so logically and happily that if ever you started a performance feeling flat, you became so caught up in the fun of it that you were exhilarated and refreshed.

At the end of *Fille* we were always so elated that I would have to quieten the company in the wings while Alexander Grant went back in his inimitable way for his red umbrella. It is typical of Ashton's genius to finish a ballet like that – subtle, and enormously touching. The first night was fantastic. We knew from rehearsals how much we had enjoyed the ballet, but the audience's response was incredible. I remember feeling tremendously elated when David Blair held me up in the air at the end of the pas de deux, and how the house seemed to explode. *NN*

ANTHONY CRICKMAY

Alexander Grant returns for his red umbrella at the very end of the ballet.

Eric Johns

Lise is to comic ballet what Giselle is to tragic ballet – a dancer's dream, though probably a dancer's nightmare during rehearsals. Small wonder that Fanny Elssler, Virginia Zucchi, Preobrazhenska, Karsavina, Pavlova, and Baronova were all eager to dance in various versions in the past. Perhaps Nadia Nerina is the most fortunate of them all, for in this first role which Ashton has created for her, he gives her unrivalled opportunities. She is alive to every one of them and even eclipses all those dazzling performances with which her career has been so profusely dotted in the past. Nerina brings a feathery abandon to her spectacular romantic pas de deux with David Blair in the first act and everything she does has an aura of artless simplicity, so entirely in keeping with the character.

– *The Stage*, 4 February 1960

Curtain call after the first night of *La Fille Mal Gardée* with Stanley Holden, David Blair, Frederick Ashton, Nadia Nerina, Osbert Lancaster, Hugo Rignold, Alexander Grant and Leslie Edwards.

Mr Ashton has here done for Nadia Nerina what he has so often done for Fonteyn. Nerina has been known as the pre-eminent technician in the company, an astonishing virtuoso, but one lacking, apparently, in the higher artistry. Mr Ashton's choreography has, in effect, added the artistry – or rather has shown Nerina herself how her very considerable technical skill may be altered from a thing in itself into a servant of lyrical dance; and the addition which that makes to the enchantment of her dance performance is enormous.

So, when all is said and done, Mr Ashton has made this, as was only right, into Nerina's ballet. And she, receiving this long-awaited gift, has done beautifully with it. Mr Ashton, we know, is in love with classicism – his every post-war ballet witnesses to that – but I do not think that he has ever before combined, quite so thoroughly, the text-book complications of classical dance with his own special taste for lyricism.

The Guardian, 30 January 1960

DANCING IN RUSSIA

It was Diaghilev who made 'Russian' the magic word for ballet and the Ballets Russes the epitome of theatrical glamour. While ballet in Russia itself remained a mysterious and legendary activity, Western dancers took Russian names, and like Lydia Sokolova, Anton Dolin, Alicia Markova, triumphed in the Ballets Russes. It was the Sadler's Wells Ballet which eventually proved that the name mattered not at all and that balletic excellence was a question of school and choreography. But the Russian magic is still potent; the visits of the Kirov and Bolshoy Ballets in the past two decades have at last shown us the reality of Russian ballet, while reciprocal appearances by Western companies and dancers have given the Russians something to ponder on. Even so, an invitation to dance in Leningrad and Moscow remains a signal honour for Western dancers and, as Konstantin Sergueyev observes in his contribution to this book, Nerina's performances as a guest with the Bolshoy and Kirov troupes were the happiest foretaste of the qualities of British ballet.

CC

WITH THE BOLSHOY AND THE KIROV

In June 1960 I was overwhelmed to receive an invitation to dance *Swan Lake* at the Bolshoy Theatre in Moscow, with the premier danseur Nikolay Fadeyechev, and to dance *Giselle* at the Kirov Theatre in Leningrad, partnered by the Company's Director, Konstantin Sergueyev. Madam was marvellous – she immediately made arrangements so that I could be free to appear in Russia in October. When the time came to go it was a tremendous rush. The Royal Ballet was on tour in America; I was in New York for three weeks for the American premiere of *Fille* and I dashed back via London en route for Moscow.

Fortunately I had some idea of their production as I had seen the Russian film of *Swan Lake* with Plisetskaya, who was exotic, glamorous and very beautiful. On my arrival I was very honoured that Marina Semyonova, a legendary ballerina, was to coach me and take all our rehearsals. I was interested to learn that it is a policy of the Bolshoy Company to allow, and indeed encourage, the ballerinas to make slight variations from the set choreography, which could enhance both their personal attributes as dancers and individual interpretations. So on occasions I was offered a choice of choreographic variation. One was Plisetskaya's, the current one; the other Mme Semyonova's. I invariably chose to learn Mme Semyonova's as it appeared that my approach was entirely in sympathy with her reading of the role of Odette/Odile.

The first class I attended was crowded and there was a marked air of tension and excitement. My technique was regarded with the utmost interest, especially my fast, neat footwork (the heritage of my Royal Ballet training) and the quick take-off for jumps. Dancers in England are swifter, lighter, and more precise than the Bolshoy artists, whose movements are more fluid and elegiac. What seemed to surprise them most was that my training embraced the characteristics of their style while retaining the attributes of the British School. The strength of the Bolshoy style emanates from the supple, strong but pliant use of the back, giving dancers a complete freedom of movement.

The next morning there was no teacher in the class. Usually in our company when this happens one of the senior boys sets the exercises – though without giving corrections – and you work alone. I presumed that they would do the same, only on this occasion a ballerina set the exercises. After *battements tendus* I was surprised at being corrected; I knew we would never correct each other in London, let alone a guest. So when I received a further correction from her and noticed the raised eyebrows of the other principals, I decided that if it happened again I would have to do something. Came the *developpés*, and again a correction. 'Niet, niet' (she wanted them fast) 'tak, tak, tak!' So I said, 'Niet, niet, developpés comme une fleur – doucement'. 'Niet', came the reply 'tak, tak, tak'. 'En Angleterre,' I said, 'doucement, doucement – comme ça.' There were no further corrections. A few amused smiles, and we continued the class uninterrupted. Of course, that was just a flash of quite understandable temperament.

Curtain call after the first performance of *Fille* in Russia: Kirov Theatre, Leningrad.

On the stage of the Bolshoy Theatre after the first performance of *Swan Lake*.

Rehearsals with Fadeyechev went easily as I had worked with him before in London in the television production of *Giselle*. The changes in Act II were minimal as this act is the same in companies the world over. In Act III I suggested that we dance the Royal Ballet version of the Black Swan, as in our production the involvement with von Rothbart in the pas de deux creates, I believe, a far more interesting dramatic situation by the interplay between the three characters. I would have to learn their entirely different Act IV, so I felt it would be a fair exchange, and interesting for the Moscow public. Mme Semyonova and Yuri Fayer, the conductor, were enthusiastic and both agreed. At the time Mr Fayer was almost blind, so when we worked on the Black Swan, where the tempi and steps were completely new to him, I held his hand and sang him through the choreography. It was incredible how he learned all the steps – like a dancer. He was a genius among ballet conductors and a very dear man, revered and loved by everyone.

In the coda they are accustomed to taking calls after each sequence of virtuosity and they were amazed when I wished to run straight through so as not to break the dramatic tension and final impact of the pas de deux. I insisted, to Fadeyechev's dismay; I even pointed out to him, 'You have plenty of time to regain your breath while I am doing the thirty-two fouettés!' In Act IV there was a great deal to learn, including numerous enormous lifts with von Rothbart. The Soviet training in the technique of partnering is meticulous and the preparatory steps before the lifts are always the same. This makes rehearsing much quicker and the lifts easier when one is tired at the end of a long evening.

During all rehearsals, at which Yuri Fayer was always present, the company were eager to help and willing to spend extra time, if necessary, on getting everything right. They were determined that I should have every confidence in my new surroundings so that I could give of my very best. Only one thing embarrassed me. Whenever I left the stage to go to my dressing room I had resin on my shoes and a lady in a white overall would follow me down the corridor with a carpet sweeper cleaning the resin off the red carpet!

The vast Bolshoy stage (half as wide again as the Royal Opera House stage) was a joy. It was a pleasure adjusting to the extra space and to the rake which I always preferred on a stage. The Bolshoy's interpretation of Tchaikovsky's score was far more expansive and lyrical, and their stress on the quality of *legato* in the musical phrasing forced one to sustain and control every movement so that one's dancing became far more fluid, fuller and broader. Yuri Fayer brought the whole production to life with natural understanding of movement and rhythm. It is this quality which makes a great ballet conductor. The late Constant Lambert had it and today, so has Ashley Lawrence, the Royal Ballet's musical director.

The reception on the first night was very warm and generous. My friend Yvette Chauviré was in Moscow at the time and was very kind and, at the end of the evening, when everyone had left my dressing room, Galina Ulanova came down and kissed me on both cheeks. I was very moved.

After my final performance in Moscow I went straight to Leningrad to dance *Giselle* at the Kirov with Konstantin Sergueyev, the illustrious premier danseur and director of the company. I was worried as there were only three days in which to rehearse. During the first morning I sensed that the company was not going to accept me on the reputation I had won in Moscow. It is not unusual to cut Giselle's mad-scene in a company rehearsal, but I knew that I must rehearse it fully with the Kirov, especially as I had not danced the role for about six months. At the end of the act, when Giselle lies dead on the floor, Sergueyev helped me to my feet without saying a word. He then dismissed the company and they all left the room silently. I was very puzzled and sat with Mrs Blackwell, my dresser who had come with me to Russia, for about twenty minutes before they all returned. Sergueyev then spoke to me through the interpreter and said that they had all been so touched by the mad-scene that he had felt it necessary for us all to take a break. From that moment their reserve faded and the rest of the rehearsal went very easily. There had always been a healthy rivalry between the Kirov and the Bolshoy and I suppose the company had decided to wait and judge me for themselves. The mad-scene had settled the matter: I was accepted.

Rehearsal next day went quickly. Sergueyev was dancing superbly and our styles blended happily. We also rehearsed with all the old machines that are used to fly Giselle through the trees and cause her to materialise precariously among the branches during the Wili scene in Act II. Mme Natalya Dudinskaya, formerly the company's prima ballerina, was most concerned when I called for a third rehearsal and later she explained that nobody ever rehearses the day before a performance and they were astounded that I had insisted on doing so.

Sergueyev at that time must have been nearly fifty but he was magnificent. He had a youthful and romantic manner, wonderful ballon, and he was a superlative partner. *NN*

Left Nadia Nerina and Maya Plisetskaya in class. **Centre** In rehearsal with Yuri Fayer. **Right** With Nikolay Fadeychev and Yuri Fayer.

NADIA NERINA'S APPEARANCES IN RUSSIA

Natalya Roslaveva, *the distinguished Russian writer on ballet*

When it became known in the early autumn of 1960 that Nadia Nerina was to dance in *Swan Lake* at the Bolshoy Theatre, the news was accepted as an event of more than ordinary importance. The Bolshoy Ballet had already danced at the Royal Opera House, Covent Garden; books had been published in Russian about the history of ballet in Great Britain; it was no longer an unknown body, and news hung in the air that a tour of the entire company was not so far away. That is why Nadia Nerina's two guest appearances at the Bolshoy attracted so much attention and interest. Realising that they were viewing one of the leading ballerinas of the Royal Ballet, both the spectators and the Bolshoy Company treated her as an envoy of British Ballet.

On her first night, dancing Odette (in Act II) she was slightly nervous, but in the fourth act she regained her self-assurance and gave a moving and eloquent performance of the suffering Odette, shielding her Prince (Nikolai Fadeyechev) in a very effective manner from the attacks of von Rothbat (Alexander Begak).

On the second night she was more composed and gave a sustained performance from the very beginning. She introduced slight changes into her costume and make-up that were more becoming to her and looked better under the Bolshoy's lights, different from those of Covent Garden. Any reservations that were voiced after the first performance concerned the part of Odette. As Odile Nerina had immediately won the approval of the Bolshoy's seasoned audience by her exceptional technique and colourful portrayal of the other side of the dual character. There were ovations in the auditorium on both occasions when Nerina introduced into Odile's coda, in Act III, an enchaînement usually performed by her in *The Sleeping Beauty*. It consisted of a *sissone ouverte* in a small arabesque, *chassé croisé* to fourth position and from there *rond de jambe sauté en dehors*.

I became so interested in this new combination of steps that I made a special trip to the Hotel National where she was staying to write it down and to ask her about it. The ballerina said that in the Royal Ballet production of *Swan Lake* she used an altogether different coda. The enchaînement in question came from *The Sleeping Beauty* and is believed to have been choreographed by Petipa. Nerina, however, gave it a more spectacular nature by introducing the 'open' effect. She explained that she danced this sequence in the third act because of the entirely different arrangement of the pas de deux and coda of *Swan Lake*, Act III, in the Covent Garden and Bolshoy versions. In Covent Garden the entire pas de deux did not break until the very end – only then was the applause taken. In the Bolshoy version (ascribed to Gorsky) the applause is taken after the fouettés, and the action proceeds after the pas de deux without interruption. Also, the entire coda, especially that of the male dancer in the second entrance, is taken at half the speed usual in London.

So it was with great taste that Nerina introduced her brilliant, fast enchaînement following immediately after Fadeyechev's coda, beautifully done in steps of elevation requiring more sustained tempo. Nerina made the entire effect through contrast of tempi, and renewed the excitement since the speed had slowed down just before her coda. This spectacular effect had a well-deserved success on both sides of the curtain. Her thirty-two fouettés, performed strictly *sur place* with great strength and speed, were also very much admired.

Many years have passed since Nadia Nerina danced for the first time at the Bolshoy, but professional memories among ballet people are still strong. I spoke recently to Professor Marina Semyonova, great ballerina of the Kirov and the Bolshoy, now ballet mistress of the Bolshoy Ballet. She rehearsed Nadia Nerina in the Bolshoy version of *Swan Lake* and had her come to her daily class. The first thing Madame Semyonova remembered when I mentioned Nerina's first performance at the Bolshoy was that very spectacular enchaînement that lent, as she rightly observed, a new kind of line to Odile's dance and was therefore interesting not merely for technical reasons. Semyonova said that Nerina's Odile was very feminine and seductive, rather than demonic, but was emotionally charged to the utmost. She especially noted Nerina's strong pointes and what she termed 'a very firm and expressive arabesque'. She said that while Nerina gave a slightly more contemporary touch to Odile's dance patterns than we were accustomed to at that time, she remained true to

Tchaikovsky's music, and that is what constituted the most important aspect of her reading of the role.

Semyonova said it was a pleasure to work with Nerina – she loved to dance, and did everything with enthusiasm and exhilaration. She added that it was easy to rehearse her in *Swan Lake* because she took work so seriously, while Nikolaí Fadeyechev, her partner, was very helpful in 'leading' the ballerina through the entire ballet and his mastery was at one with the abilities of his ballerina. In speaking to me recently Semyonova also recalled Nerina's appearances as Lise in the Royal Ballet's *La Fille Mal Gardée* in the summer of the next year. Her Lise, said Semyonova, was perfection itself – lyrical, playful, temperamental – she had all the qualities required by this very difficult role. 'Time', she said 'has not erased my memories of Nadia Nerina.'

But to return to Nadia's debut at the Bolshoy. When the curtain closed for the last time, the entire ballet company and members of other 'shops' – dressers, designers, stage managers, etc. – assembled on the huge stage. The late Professor Leonid Lavrovsky, Director of the Bolshoy Ballet and its principal choreographer, congratulated the guest ballerina on her great and deserved success. He emphasised that the warm reception on the part of the Bolshoy Ballet to Nadia Nerina was due not only to her being a talented artist but also because she proved to be such a warm-hearted and genuine person.

The Royal Ballet's arrival in Moscow in 1961: Frederick Ashton, Graham Usher, Galina Ulanova, Donald McLeary and Nadia Nerina.

The Kirov Theatre Leningrad on the first night of the Royal Ballet's visit. Seated in the box from left: Michael Wood, Dame Ninette de Valois, Sir Frank Roberts the British Ambassador, John Hart, Sir David Webster, Lady Roberts, Sir Frederick Ashton.

The next day Nadia Nerina was off to Leningrad where she took part in two performances of *Giselle* – on Sunday, 30 October and on Wednesday, 2 November – both at the Kirov Theatre, with its blue and gold auditorium and the wonderful curtain painted by Golovin in the same colour-scheme. She had an overwhelming success on both occasions. Armfuls of flowers were thrown upon the stage after the first act and there were so many curtain calls that she thought for a while that *Giselle* in Leningrad must end there. But the second act followed in due course and with it another ovation. The audience clapped in time as is customary in Soviet theatres on occasions when the artist is very much admired. Of course, a considerable part of this admiration was reflected by the personality of Konstantin Sergeyev, Nerina's illustrious partner. He was then still the Kirov Ballet's premier danseur and his very large following felt admiration for the ballerina he chose to dance with.

Nerina found the Leningrad production of *Giselle* similar to the one she was accustomed to in the Royal Ballet with only some slight additions in music and mime and a greater variety of stage effects in Act II. After her second *Giselle* Nerina literally had to cut the curtain calls, in order to catch the midnight 'Red Arrow' train to Moscow.

We next saw Nerina in the summer of 1961 when she came with the Royal Ballet. The company was greatly appreciated by the Kirov and Bolshoy audiences for the seriousness of its artistic purpose and the attitude of each and every one of its members to the art they love. The company was recognised as having a distinct style of its own, its repertoire was found to be very interesting and representative of British traditions in art and theatre. The interest was, I should say, centred on choreography rather than on interpretation, though it goes without saying that the constellation of the Royal Ballet ballerinas was highly acclaimed. The first half of the tour took place in Leningrad where Nerina was received as an artist already known to the public. Vera Krasovskaya, one of the leading Leningrad critics, said that Nerina, 'who had already charmed our audiences in

Giselle during her first visit to Leningrad with her light, uninhibited and clear-cut dancing, endeared herself to us in the role of Lise'. 'It is', said Krasovskaya, 'closer to her individual talents. Her coquetry is so artlessly naive, her joy and sorrows so openhearted. It looks as if the pranks of Lise-Nerina are born on the spot, and that the sun smiles through a cloud when Lise, who had just been spanked by her mother, plots new mischief, smiling through her tears.' Krasovskaya noted that Nerina and Blair formed a perfect partnership in the same light lyrical comedy manner. They fully understood one another, not only because the story called for such a spirit, but, competing in virtuosity, each of them complemented the other's dancing.

Krasovskaya, herself a former dancer, found that Nerina 'has been born for the dance and dancing is her joy. The most difficult passages seem to hold no difficulties for her. She is complete master of her body. This enables her to execute any technical feats with the utmost ease and exhilaration. Probably that remarkable Russian ballerina, Olga Preobrazhenskaya, danced like this – her dance was also as musical and as unrestrained as a song.'

The Moscow visit opened at the Bolshoy on 2 July 1961. Nerina appeared for the first time on 4 July in *La Fille Mal Gardée*. It is difficult to put into words her personal success, inseparable from the overall impression made by Ashton's masterpiece. One thing was fully realised – he could not have created it without the brilliance of Nerina's special talent. Ashton's choreographic invention in this ballet is inexhaustible. Take the moment when Lise, holding in her raised hands a bunch of pink ribbons becomes an improvised maypole, slowly performing a complete *tour en attitude* on the point of one foot. This calls for virtuosity of the highest order and it required a ballerina of no lesser calibre than Nadia Nerina. Or take the absolutely delightful tiny *taqueté* steps, repeated twice *en diagonale*, that give such a French flavour to this otherwise thoroughly British ballet. The Moscow critic Yelizaveta Suritz made special note of this particular enchaînement, calling it 'Lise's charming run *sur les pointes*, with the feet thrown forward – both coquettish, elegant and a trifle mocking; it serves as an excellent dance characterisation for her found by Ashton through an unusual application of known steps'. Suritz said that the general dance style of the Royal Ballet abounded in purity of line nobility of form and a certain reserve in manner. 'Not for a moment did any of them, not even the most technical, Nadia Nerina, forget that outward impressions do not determine the quality of dancing. That is why nobody turned endless fouettés with distorted faces – as one sees at times – in order to reach the sacred figure of thirty-two.'

Aside from her virtuosity, Nerina's acting in *La Fille Mal Gardée* met with the highest praise. We believed in every scene, we came to love her lively and gay Lise. How could I ever forget that moment when Lise blows her nose after having cried in the scene with Colas, only to be laughing and smiling a minute later. Nikolai Eliash, the prominent Moscow critic, said in his article: 'Nerina's virtuosity in *La Fille Mal Gardée* is coloured by the proper degree of characterisation that creates here the necessary feeling of youth, unbridled ease, and slight naughtiness. I would like to add that Nerina in *La Fille Mal Gardée* showed not merely feats of virtuosity but performed a very amusing mimed scene with great humour. She danced with equal success the gay and witty Lise and the mysterious, quivering, impetuous Firebird in Stravinsky's ballet.'

The great Bolshoy premier danseur, Mikhail Gabovich, who at that time had already acquired a considerable reputation as a writer on ballet, said that Nerina was 'an excellent ballerina, whose graceful, technically perfect dance was already known to Muscovites after her recent tour'. Commenting on Nerina's appearance in *The Firebird* Gabovich said it was a pleasure to see how she, together with the entire ensemble, endeavoured to convey the special features of Russian dance. I remember how, in speaking to me about Nerina's technique, Gabovich said that as well as being obviously a ballerina in her own right, Nerina was in many ways very close to our school – she had better placing of the body, more expressive *ports de bras*, and the approach to her roles showed an attempt to reach a complete identification, in the spirit of the Russian school. Gabovich valued Nerina's special quality of aerial lightness very highly.

Her full technical brilliance was revealed in *The Sleeping Beauty*. It was universally agreed that all the three Auroras were outstanding in their own way, but Nerina's was the most sparkling. Small, fair, graceful, her Aurora radiated special charm.

Royal Ballet class in the Kirov Theatre, Leningrad: among the dancers are Annette Page, Margot Fonteyn, Nadia Nerina and Georgina Parkinson.

Russia was an extremely interesting experience. The Russians loved *Fille*, and the whole cast had a very big success. They admired Nadia Nerina: she had the qualities that they look for – an easy soft jump, flow of arm movement and strong feet. I think that Russia thought highly of all our ballets; the main thing that they could not understand was how we could have done it all in the time! They could not comprehend how it was only thirty years since the beginnings of the company.

Dame Ninette de Valois

ZOE DOMINIC

NADIA NERINA'S GISELLE

Konstantin Sergueyev, *People's Artist of the USSR*

Though more than ten years have passed since that memorable event, I still recall most vividly how, in the summer of 1961, the Kirov Ballet danced for the first time at the Royal Opera House while simultaneously the Royal Ballet opened its tour on the Kirov stage in Leningrad. This event roused considerable interest in the Russian theatrical world, for we had not seen the British national ballet, though of course some of us knew about it. We realised the considerable gulf that separated us as far as age and tradition were concerned, yet there was something in common between us.

The Royal Ballet brought an authentic version of *The Sleeping Beauty*, born on this very stage; and I know that London still remembers the triumphs achieved by such great artists as Anna Pavlova, Vaslav Nijinsky, Mikhail Fokine and Tamara Karsavina, in the first seasons of the Diaghilev Ballet. Later many other Maryinsky-trained dancers enabled Diaghilev to revive classical ballet in all its splendour through the 1921 London production of *The Sleeping Princess*. These historical details show that the ties between our schools, though indirect, are of long standing and had been maturing over a period of years. When the Royal Ballet showed its production of *The Sleeping Beauty* at the Kirov Theatre, these proximities became obvious.

The Royal Ballet had an overwhelming and deserved success in Leningrad, while simultaneously the Kirov Ballet was being applauded in London. Since I was in London I was unable to witness the success attained by the Royal Ballet ballerinas, but I was fully informed about the ovations that accompanied the performances of Nadia Nerina, who had charmed both the professionals and the general public in Ashton's *La Fille Mal Gardée* and in *The Sleeping Beauty*. This success was partly due to the fact that Nerina was already an old favourite: a few months before the arrival of the Royal Ballet she had flown to the banks of the Neva as its first messenger, a Spring swallow, even though in reality it was late in October.

Nerina was invited to dance in our *Giselle*, and I was asked to partner her. The role of Albrecht has always been one of my favourites and has accompanied me throughout my entire theatrical life. I started my career with this role in 1928, and in this very role I appeared for the last time before the public in 1962. I seldom changed my Giselles. My first on the Kirov stage was Galina Ulanova; I had the honour of dancing *Giselle* with Elena Lukom; and my last Giselle, with whom I danced uninterruptedly for many years, was Natalya Dudinskaya.

I consider partnership in pas de deux to be a matter of the greatest importance. Unity of style, mutual understanding, school – all should help to enhance the inner significance of the roles. This complexity of problems and a feeling of responsibility made me very much aware of the difficulties in meeting with a new Giselle, in this case Nadia Nerina. At the same time, as the then premier danseur of the Kirov ballet, I felt it my duty to be of maximum assistance to our guest-artist.

My first encounter with Nadia Nerina could not leave me indifferent. This was more than a meeting of my Albrecht with a new Giselle: it was an encounter of a disciple of the Leningrad school with a stranger from Cape Town, now ballerina of the Royal Ballet.

Yet everything was surprisingly simple. Nadia's personal charm was most engaging; her kind, trusting and lively eyes aroused in me a responsive feeling of friendliness, and she turned out to be a delightful guest. My knowledge of French appeared to be quite adequate, although Albrecht's encounters with Giselle need no words, and we conversed in the idiom of the *danse d'ècole*.

Why did we understand one another so easily in *Giselle*? I am confident that it was because the version existing in the repertory of the Royal Ballet since the early thirties is our Russian *Giselle* in a version produced by the great master, Marius Petipa, for the Maryinsky ballet. It was Petipa who created the *grand pas* of the Wilis, and gave many other touches to the second act. And it was many generations of Russian ballerinas and premiers danseurs who lent our *Giselle* its uninterrupted life. Nikolay Sergeyev revived the Maryinsky *Giselle* for Sadler's Wells Ballet in 1934, and with some production nuances the choreography remains the same. Thus there was no question of learning a new 'text'; any

Konstantin Sergueyev and Nadia Nerina in *Giselle*.

questions arose merely in connection with some details in the *mise-en-scène* and individual interpretations.

But there was something else that made the success of our rapport in this ballet so complete. Rather unexpectedly Nadia Nerina's entire manner of dancing turned out to be very much like that of the Leningrad school, and in *Giselle* she was particularly close to it. This became evident in the course of the very first rehearsals, taken in the famous two-tiered rehearsal hall in Rossi Street. I took the rehearsal, showing some of our *mise-en-scène* to Nadia, and merging our own solos in a unified ensemble; in other words, I was faced by the task of making her into one of us, but after the second rehearsal our duo was quite organic. We understood one another easily, and reacted readily to the slightest changes in the readings of the characters, the phrasing, rhythm and any special shading in the execution of the steps.

I can say without any exaggeration that I did not even have to try and 'accommodate' myself to my new partner. *Giselle* is the kind of ballet where the success of the duos is determined not merely by the accord in movement, unity of technique, a feeling for the Romantic style. The harmony of pas de deux is reached through insights into the dramatics of the ballet and its psychological content. In the second act the pas de deux are mostly based on adagio tempi, and are rich in lifts, both *par terre* and *en l'air*, but in Act I, in order to reach accord in the duos, one should be well versed in allegro, not to mention mime, in order to achieve a proper reading and understanding of the act.

It was most pleasant to dance with Nadia Nerina in Act I, because she showed mastery of all these aspects, and when jumping her elevation was almost as high as that of a man.

In the second act she created for us an ethereal, phantom Giselle; her brilliant technique captivated our spectators, and her very first appearance in Act II, when she performed the tempestuous *temps levés en arabesque en tournant*, was immediately followed by a transition *sur les pointes* in fifth position, in which pose she continued to turn. Thus she introduced something of her own, without infringing on the general style and texture of the ballet.

She was always ready to meet our requests. I succeeded in persuading Nadia to try the big lifts used by us in Act II, when Albrecht holds the ballerina for a moment, arms raised to the utmost, and keeps the pose, enhancing the illusion of sustained flight. This is a difficult lift, but Nadia risked it and carried everything off to perfection: it looked as if I was trying to restrain Giselle from flying away! This type of lift, which has long been a tradition for all our performers in *Giselle*, had first been introduced by that great couple, Elena Lukom and Boris Shavrov, in the 1920s.

One could say many other things about Nadia's Giselle. Her reading of the role and her very individual manner of performance were new for our spectators. She combined buoyancy, even expansiveness, with great softness, lyricism and a touch of naiveté. Her execution of the 'mad' scene moved both the audience and cast: she slightly distorted the purity of the classical line (but to an extent that did not interfere with the general beauty of plastique) and used this broken line to portray her heroine's deranged mind. It was touching to see her body double up like a flower bent by the wind; it was a body that had lost its willpower and the very instinct for life, and Nadia conveyed this purely through dance pattern. There was nothing pathological in her 'mad' scene, she did not introduce any everyday gestures. It was all done *plastically*. Even the rather free treatment of traditional patterns was more than justified, since it served its purpose.

In our time Galina Ulanova and I tried hard to free *Giselle* from the burden of conventional gesture, replacing it with expressive acting, so that hardly any conventional mime is used in our modern performances of *Giselle*. But we did not infringe upon Nerina's customary way of performance, letting her act the mimed scenes as she was accustomed to, and carefully reacting in her style. The differences were very small, and mostly concerned Giselle's first encounter with Albrecht.

In Act I Nerina danced Giselle's first variation with such lightness, speed and brio that she immediately endeared herself to our audience. It was she who, figuratively speaking, 'lifted the curtain' to show us a little of the Royal Ballet; it goes without saying that the people of Leningrad greeted her as an old friend when the Royal Ballet visited us in the summer of 1961.

The Rose Adagio at the Bolshoy during the Royal Ballet's visit to Moscow.

NERINA IN LENINGRAD

Natalya Dudinskaya, *People's Artist of the USSR*

I remember the very beginning of the 1960–61 season when, in the course of Sergueyev's work with our guest-artist Nadia Nerina, I was asked to show her our version of the ending of *Giselle*, Act II. Two things surprised me straightaway: how spontaneous Nadia Nerina's reaction was to anything new, and how close the substance of her school was to ours. To my knowledge most of the western schools pay greater attention to technique for the feet and legs and much less to the work of the hands, arms, and body. But in the case of Nadia Nerina, she danced with all of her body. Her *port de bras* was strikingly like that of the Russian school.

Among her other qualities I was very much impressed by her 'weightlessness' when she jumped. It had a unique resilient quality. One often comes across a jump that is light enough, but, lacking *ballon*, it does not have the bouncy quality of falling and rising, as if being thrown off the ground. Nerina was in full possession of this rare gift which also made it easier for her to hold a pose in the air – and this is of special importance in the dance patterns of *Giselle* as we understand it.

As one who had danced the part of Giselle on many occasions, I was most moved and greatly impressed by her 'mad' scene. It was carried out with the help of broken lines of the body, expressing the broken state of Giselle's inner being. There were other aspects too. Nadia Nerina succeeded in the earlier part of Act I in conveying Giselle's exhilaration, her joy in seeing the world around her; and these qualities of spontaneity were of great help in her work with Sergueyev.

Partnership is far from a simple problem and one that does not grow overnight. Konstantin Sergueyev's great experience enabled him to guide Nadia Nerina, and she soon grasped the substance of our interpretation so that their duet was organic and real.

Nerina also came to my daily company class. There were of course some points and aspects quite new to her; as a pupil of Agrippina Vaganova I conduct a class strictly according to her method. It is, figuratively speaking, in my bones – I was at school under Vaganova for three years, and then for twenty more, uninterruptedly, I attended her company class. All the leading Kirov ballerinas came to this *classe de perfectionnement* and it goes without saying that on the day Nerina came to join us, the lesson was not made any easier. Yet Nadia was exceptionally quick in catching up with everything.

I consider her to be one of the most brilliant members of the constellation of ballerinas produced by the British National ballet, and it is regrettable that the stage lost her much too early. When she came to Leningrad in January 1973 to take part in my jubilee the audience recognised her in the auditorium of the Philharmonic Hall and a great ovation broke out.

Above Natalya Dudinskaya and Konstantin Sergueyev in the Kirov production of *The Sleeping Beauty*. **Right** *Firebird* at the Bolshoy.

The Berceuse – the Firebird casts a spell to put all Kastchey's creatures to sleep.

FIREBIRD

At first I found it difficult to interpret *Firebird*, but Dame Ninette gave me an instant and vivid direction when she talked about the magical quality of the bird, with 'fingers like sparks in the air'. It is an exhilarating role to dance, but the first scene is the most tiring in the whole ballet repertory. The Firebird enters with two sequences of flying jetés across the stage, followed immediately by a solo of continuous jumps which must not appear to the audience to be anywhere near as tiring as they are. This leads, without a pause, into a long pas de deux, where the choreography demands many soaring lifts and runs as the Firebird fights desperately to free herself from her captor. Finally, after this breathless chase, Ivan catches her triumphantly, and during a long and very lovely passage, slowly lowers her down on to her knees, bending her backwards so that he may gaze into her face. It is at this precise moment that the dancer most needs to regain her breath, but in the back-bent position it is impossible and there are only a few seconds in which one can gasp before the Firebird struggles free and flies off into the night. *NN*

The Firebird caught by Ivan Tsarevitch (Michael Somes).

FIREBIRD IN MOSCOW

David Blair

I think that the first *Fille* in Leningrad was even more exciting than the London première. There is a wonderful ballet public in Leningrad, a tradition of one hundred and fifty years of balletomania, and in the summer the fans go out into the fields and pick wild flowers which they wrap in paper and soak in water; they are not supposed to bring them into the theatre, but somehow they do, and if they like you, they throw these flowers all through the performance. It happened on the first night just after I had finished my first variation, and I wondered what on earth was going on – were they throwing cabbages? Then we realised, and we had to clear the stage of flowers before the next dances could take place. From then on it was a series of showers of flowers: the audience were enchanted – they understood all about the technical difficulties and they were fantastically responsive.

It was tremendous to dance at the Kirov, the old Maryinsky Theatre: one could sense the presence of Legnani and Karsavina, Nijinsky and Fokine, and the smell of grease-paint and the dust carried memories of the past. The very fact of being on that great stage sent one's adrenalin racing.

It was not quite the same in Moscow; the city is far more 'touristy', and the real Moscow ballet public did not seem to show up except for one Sunday morning performance which turned out to be quite extraordinary. Nadia and Michael Somes were appearing in *The Firebird*, and this was the first time the original version had been seen in Russia. The company were giving a superb performance; the orchestra was fine, and obviously adored the music. When the last scene came, the reaction was amazing. The Bolshoy is only five minutes away from the Kremlin, whose fantastic domes were painted on the back-drop, and when, in the last scene, Ivan Tsarevich was crowned, the whole audience seemed to roar with delight at the splendour of their own history which was being shown by an English company.

After the final performance of *Firebird* at the Bolshoy. Members of the Royal Ballet include, from left: Svetlana Beriosova, John Lanchbery, Frederick Ashton, Nadia Nerina, Michael Somes, Dame Ninette de Valois, Brian Shaw, Emmanuel Young, Ronald Hynd and Ray Powell. The programme had also included *The Lady and the Fool* and *Les Patineurs*.

REHEARSAL AND CLASS

Like an iceberg, the visible part of a ballet performance is but one tenth of a whole. In the auditorium of a theatre we are hardly aware of the immense amount of discipline and hard work that goes into even the briefest pas de deux – the morning of rehearsal that may produce just one minute of choreography, the daily class that every dancer must submit to, the constant labours of répétiteurs and ballet staff to keep a large company repertory at performance peak. The dancer's daily battle in class is unceasing, the instrument never as near perfection as either dancer or teacher dare hope, nor will it ever be; every stage appearance demands additional sweated labour on both mechanics and matters of interpretation; the more senior a dancer becomes in a company, the greater the demands and the responsibilities and the travail. For the classical ballerina there can never be any real surcease from this toil, and certainly never any complacency about her work: corrections in class every morning are a great antidote to applause. Dancers are remarkable not least for their humility in the face of their art and, as Nerina observes, any relaxation of professional tensions is impossible save during an annual holiday. The dancer's life really demands the combined temperaments of an Olympic athlete and a member of a religious order: without both physical stamina and unquestioning dedication, nothing worthwhile is possible on stage. CC

When you find a fault it may take months to correct in daily class with a teacher, but when you have corrected it, you are freed from some sort of worry and you have added to your performance. Each new teacher can open up fresh areas of doubt; one is always questioning and correcting. *NN*

ACQUIRING TECHNIQUE

Acquiring technique is never easy, though I was lucky in having an 'easy body'; since I had been given this instrument I felt it was up to me to make it better. Not better than anybody else, but better than myself yesterday. I was influenced and inspired by other dancers – one always gains by watching other artists – but I was in competition only with myself.

It is vital for a dancer to understand her body completely and to know how it works. The correct use of the muscles ensures that no movement ever looks heavy. A leg is light if it is lifted by its own muscles, without displacing any other part of the body. One's mental attitude to dance is very important; if you think 'tense' you will dance tensely and an interpretation will be upset. You must be master of your body in order to dance freely; you have to train your arms and legs to hold their own weight, to work with their own muscles. You must learn to move 'in one piece', quickly and easily, so that nothing is 'left behind'. When you balance you must know exactly what is happening everywhere in your body.

Working in front of a mirror in class, I always felt that I was teaching and correcting someone I did not know. It was rather like training another person, and when something needed work I would try it time and again and often feel 'why can't she do it?' about the dancer seen in the mirror. But there is a danger in working too much to the mirror; one tends to concentrate more on the visual image and less on inward control. Company class was always held in a mirrored studio, but in my private lessons I hardly ever used the mirror. Of course the body is never fully trained: there will always be more to learn. *NN*

ANTHONY CRICKMAY

Rehearsing *Laurentia* with Rudolf Nureyev.

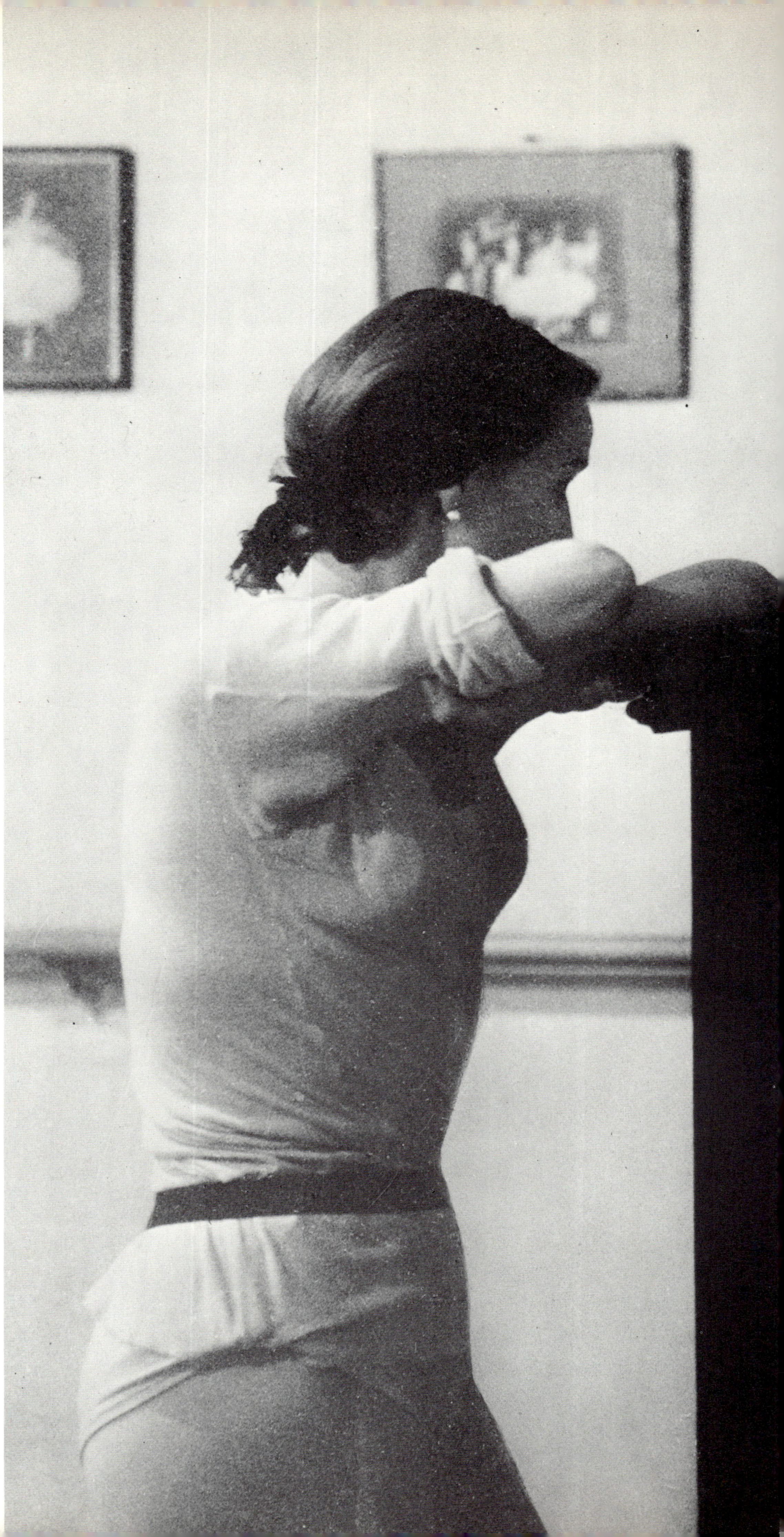

With Hilda Gaunt, tireless
rehearsal-pianist of the Royal Ballet.

ANTHONY CRICKMAY

Now That I have given up dancing I realise how involved I was in performances, how totally bound up in my roles. I did not think I could ever give up dancing: it was like a drug. I seldom went away for weekends as the break would interrupt my involvement; apart from holidays I never stopped studying and thinking about my work. *NN*

Yvette Chauviré teaching the *Grand Pas Classique* to Nerina and Blair at the Royal Ballet School.

ANTHONY CRICKMAY

Kenneth MacMillan rehearsing Nadia Nerina in his *Images of Love* for the Shakespeare quartercentenary celebrations in 1964. **Above** with Anthony Dowell. **Top** with Keith Rosson **Below** with Desmond Doyle. **Opposite** Attilio Labis, a premier danseur of the Paris Opéra, rehearsing *Swan Lake* Act II with Nadia Nerina, during his guest appearances with the Royal Ballet in 1964.

ANTHONY CRICKMAY

BALLETS AND GUESTS AT COVENT GARDEN

The Royal Ballet has been remarkably successful in building a balletic repertory proper to a great national company. From the very beginnings the basic 'classics' were staged as an example and academy for dancers and audience. Parallel with this went the necessary building of a native ballet tradition, first in the works of Ninette de Valois, and then in the ballets of Frederick Ashton which did so much to give an identity to the English style of dancing, in both one-act works and in the full-length ballets which came as a logical, national development of the acquired Petipa manner, from Cinderella *in 1948, through* Ondine *and* La Fille Mal Gardée. *From these works and the classics there came the inspiration for Ashton's heirs – John Cranko in his* Prince of the Pagodas *(1957) and the big ballets he was later to make for his Stuttgart company, and Kenneth MacMillan with* Romeo and Juliet, Anastasia *and* Manon.

A further duty devolved upon the Sadler's Wells Ballet, even in its early days: that of preserving the most important works of the twentieth century, specifically those of the Diaghilev era. The Folkine masterpieces were soon mounted, and the post-war years have seen the acquisition of the foremost examples of work by Massine and Nijinska.

But it is important that a company should also be open to the creativity of the major choreographers of the day, and the Royal Ballet can today boast some of the best works of Tudor, Balanchine, Robbins and Glen Tetley, among others. The example of outstanding guest artists must also be noted in the enriching of the company: dancers such as Danilova, Markova, Chauviré, Makarova, Dolin, Massine, Bruhn and Nureyev have been seen to great advantage. The results of this catholicity of taste have been entirely beneficial; no company in the world has so wide-ranging a repertory; none has artists so appreciative of different styles, able within the space of a week to deal magnificently with the very different demands of Petipa, Ashton, MacMillan, Tetley and Nijinska. CC

The opulent sets and costumes by Eugene Berman were magnificent. Dancing in this evocative set made one feel as if in an imperial court and the music helped in this too. The most difficult thing in the ballet was the walk round the stage when the courtiers bow to you; to get the right 'feel', I imagined there was a long regal cloak trailing behind me. Difficult too was the majestic walk in the slow movement – it was emotionally moving to bourrée forward and go into the deep arabesque with the cavalier. At the end of this movement there is an extended exit. It was essential to keep the audience's attention with you. You could not exit and think, 'Well, that's over', because it is a very long bourrée to the back of the stage and the wings and the whole atmosphere could drop. I found it very satisfying on those evenings when I knew I had maintained the tension. When the ballet was revived with the new blue costumes and decor which Mr Balanchine wanted, I never enjoyed it so much; with the Berman designs it felt right immediately. In Leningrad, standing in the great hall of the Winter Palace, with massive gold columns and huge chandeliers, I got exactly the same feeling as I had had in *Ballet Imperial*.

NN

Above and right With David Blair in *Ballet Imperial*: choreography by George Balanchine: music, Tchaikovsky's second piano concerto; costumes in this production by Carl Toms.

NOCTAMBULES

Noctambules: with choreography by Kenneth MacMillan, score by Humphrey Searle, scenery and costumes by Nicholas Georgiadis; first performed at Covent Garden on 1 March 1956. Nadia Nerina danced the role of the Faded Beauty, Leslie Edwards the Hypnotist, Maryon Lane his Assistant, Anya Linden the Poor Girl, Desmond Doyle the Rich Boy, and Brian Shaw the Soldier.

Andrew Porter

In his two ballets for the junior company at Sadler's Wells, Mr MacMillan had already shown that he was the most interesting, the most alive of our choreographers. Danses Concertantes *was a brilliant patterning to Stravinsky's music;* House of Birds *was more ambitious, wider-ranging, if a less complete, fusion of sight and sound (for Mompou's soft-centred music provided the score).*

In both of these ballets Mr MacMillan worked with the young Greek designer Nicholas Georgiadis – worked hand-in-glove, so that each ballet sprang from dancing and décor alike. In Noctambules *the same pair has been joined by Humphrey Searle, composer of the music; and so completely integrated is the result that after one performance it is hard to attribute the credit for some of the most striking theatrical effects.*

'Noctambules' *means sleep-walkers, but these characters are not sleep-walkers in the fashion of Balanchine's* Somnambule. *The scene is a little variety theatre in the back-streets. The hypnotist's act misfires, the audience mock him, and he hypnotises them all; then the rich dance with the poor, the seedy private becomes a hero, the faded beauty regains her looks – until the show is over! It is a good scenario (Mr MacMillan's own) – a scenario which allows of romance, of the glory and pathos of wish-fulfilment, and finally, of gently realistic disillusion. And to spark the tale into poetry Mr MacMillan has the hypnotist fall in love with the Beauty, whose beauty must fade when he lifts the spell.*

As a sculptor sees, latent within a block of marble, the form that he can release from it, so (if we may allow a loose metaphor) Mr MacMillan has provided his chief interpreters with contemporary roles that spring from all that they have done best before. Mr Brian Shaw, admired in so many vigorous variations, now finds his perfect one in his role of the Soldier. Mr Desmond Doyle, a fluent romantic dancer, is at last perfectly suited as the rich youth who waltzes in a half-trance with a poor girl, admirably danced by Miss Anya Linden. Miss Maryon Lane (who, as the hypnotist's assistant, finds a role analogous to Nicklaus in Hoffman – the only person not caught up in the spell) finds her incisive and very individual gifts employed more effectively than ever before.

And in the part of the Beauty, Mr MacMillan has created a genuine ballerina role, which allows full scope to Miss Nadia Nerina – there is even a kind of modern derivative of the Rose Adagio.

– *The Financial Times*, 2 March 1956

G.B.L. WILSON

The Faded Beauty and the Hypnotist.

G.B.L. WILSON

Pas de Cinq with Gary Burne, Christopher Newton,
Ronald Plaisted, Derek Rencher, and Leslie Edwards as the Hypnotist.

I thought Nadia was astounding when she did her first *Sleeping Beauty* – it was a very youthful interpretation, but superb, and when I came to create *Noctambules* I wanted to make a modern Rose Adagio for her, because even then she had all the technique of a grand ballerina. So I made an adagio for her with four boys: her body could do anything, and I was particularly concerned to reveal her speed and her wonderful jump.

Kenneth MacMillan

Les Rendezvous. Nadia Nerina and Brian Shaw in Ashton's ballet to Auber music with designs by William Chappel.

Scènes de Ballet with choreography by Frederick Ashton, music by Stravinsky and designs by André Beaurepaire.

ONDINE

Ondine was scheduled to come back to the repertoire in February 1964, and I was overjoyed when Ashton asked me to learn it. There was no recording of Hans Werner Henze's beautiful score, and I had to rehearse to a scratchy tape which had been made abroad, shortly after the music had been completed, by an orchestra which had only sight-read the score. It sounded exactly as if it had been recorded in Grand Central Station.

Ondine is a marvellous role to dance, but it is long – one is on stage most of the time. Margot Fonteyn was able to give me some rehearsal, but it was Michael Somes – who has a wonderful memory – who really taught me the part. My key to understanding the role was that Ondine, half sprite and half woman, is really more in love with her own feminine form than with Palemon, the hero. *NN*

James Kennedy

If Ondine *fails to keep a place in the Royal Ballet's repertory, that should not be for lack of a successor to Fonteyn in the main role. Nerina proved that quite sufficiently last night at Covent Garden.* Ondine *is, of all ballets, the one most sedulously made in Fonteyn's image and Nerina the virtuoso is, of all the top dancers in the Royal Ballet, the one who is usually regarded as being most dissimilar from Fonteyn the lyricist.*

But the account she gave of Ondine last night was beyond question beautiful; she caught and kept its mood, and that air of brilliant technical assurance which comes so readily to her was never allowed to obtrude – her movements caught and kept the almost liquid gentleness of style which is proper to Sir Frederick Ashton's naiad. Your purist could point out that certain gestures and postures, which in Fonteyn seem as to the manner born, appear in Nerina to be less spontaneous. Yet these were only slight limitations in a performance which showed that a dancer who has such technical strength and so balletic a physique and who is so dedicated to her task, could conquer almost any role. Her partner was Desmond Doyle, always a model of helpful tact.

– *The Guardian,* 21 February 1964

Ondine. Choreography by Ashton, score by Hans Werner Henze and designs by Lila de Nobili.
Nadia Nerina as Ondine and Alexander Grant as Tirrenio in Act III.

The shipwreck scene, *Ondine* Act II.

Robert Helpmann rehearsing *Elektra*.

ELEKTRA

Sir Robert Helpmann

Dame Ninette originally asked me to arrange a pas de deux for Nadia for a gala, but I explained to Nadia that I am not that sort of a 'steps' choreographer and that I strongly suspected that because she was so good in comedy she could be a fine dramatic artist: I had seen signs of this in her Giselle. I had long had a plan at the back of my mind to create a whole work about the *Oresteia*, to be called 'The Web of the Eumenides', and I thought that the *Elektra* section would be very good for Nadia.

She did not seem entirely convinced of my image of her, but she proved wonderful to work with, particularly since I wanted to have Elektra thrown about to illustrate the helplessness of the girl in the power of the Furies. I was not aiming at acrobatics, but Elektra had to be literally thrown by the Fates – and this was the whole point of the ballet, which a lot of critics seem to misunderstand.

I have since restaged the ballet with several other ballerinas in Australia, but none has been quite so exhilarating to work with: Nadia was willing to attempt any feat of daring. The lifts and throws we tried out in rehearsal were not new to me as I had learnt them as a very young man when I worked in musical comedies.

Nadia understood my intention to portray in dance the sexual ferocity that is in the play, and our work was a true collaboration. She was like a whirlwind. I would love to have a metronome reading of Nadia's performance because I still have to say to dancers, very good ones too, 'Nadia did it quicker than that!' The ballet was well-received in New York – unlike some of the London notices – but the most gratifying thing was that Martha Graham came to the first night and was absolutely thrilled with it, and with Nadia. She thought her a sensation: 'Oh, what a waste of a great modern dancer', was her comment.

Elektra, with choreography by Robert Helpmann, score by Malcolm Arnold, scenery and costumes by Arthur Boyd, and lighting by William Bundy, was first performed by the Royal Ballet at Covent Garden on 26 March 1963. Nadia Nerina danced the role of Elektra, David Blair that of Orestes, and Monica Mason and Derek Rencher were Clytemnestra and Aegisthus.

The Illustrated London News commented: ' ... it proceeds at a breakneck and sensational pace through a series of ingenious, dramatic and highly tense lifts, solos and ensembles. It may not be Aeschylean – it is certainly very exciting and received a resounding ovation on the first night.'

Elektra was given its American premiere in New York on 14 May 1963, at the Metropolitan Opera House.

I had been to Greece and seen a performance of *Elektra* with Katina Paxinou, which was profoundly moving. When Robert Helpmann asked me to dance Elektra for him, I was rather unsure: I was blonde and felt I was probably not right for the part. I asked him if he was sure of his choice, because I had never played anything so 'dark' in emotional colouring. Helpmann just told me, 'Don't think about it; it is going to last twenty minutes and you are on stage all the time and the tension has got to last from beginning to end.' Malcolm Arnold's score had a tremendously strong pulse, which forced one on. As we got into rehearsals, Helpmann told me that the two groups of four boys he was using for the Furies were to throw me about in the air. I have always trusted my partners so I trusted these eight boys too – I never doubted they would catch me. The throws evolved at rehearsals, and each day we would find ways of tossing me further and higher; there was one moment when I flew upside down from one side of the stage to the other. There was no rest at all, because even when Orestes was doing his variation I was crouching on the floor sustaining the tension, rather like a cat waiting to spring at a bird. *NN*

HOUSTON ROGERS

Nerina as Elektra, Blair as Orestes with Monica Mason and Derek Rencher as Clytemnestra and Aegisthus, 1963.

Orestes and Elektra.

After some sixteen years Mr Robert Helpmann has returned to Covent Garden as the choreographer of a new ballet. Its theme is that of Aeschylus's Elektra *and it was thunderously welcomed at its first performance last night.*

Helpmann's version of Elektra *will, nevertheless, sharply divide ballet-goers and it is as well to summarise the intentions and the premises. It is a dance-drama rather than a ballet, some quarter of an hour in duration yet leisurely in effect though the atmosphere is intense. The style is theatrical and spectacular: the initial exposition calls loudly for attention, not only in Malcolm Arnold's vociferous orchestral baying but in Arthur Boyd's hysterical and immensely striking line-drawings of anatomical nightmares, black upon white, all eyes and teeth and thighs and hair behind a blood-red floorcloth upon which Elektra (Nadia Nerina) sits cross-legged, the fatal hatchet lifted above her doom-red hair, eight male Furies, blue and yellow, spread-eagled supine before her.*

Before long she has been thrown up and down and along, like a milliner's bale of material, she has spun and writhed and grovelled maniacally, been hoisted up and over Orestes' shoulders (David Blair at his most muscular and dynamic), until finally, after the chopper has been swung lethally at Clytemnestra and her unusually robust paramour (Monica Mason and Derek Rencher, whose cohabitation is represented with grim relish) Elektra is left caressing and mooning over the gory weapon, while Orestes is crucified upside-down by the Furies, and then nailed to the ground.

The method is mordant and dynamic and provocative, a reaction from line and fluidity in favour of blunt, physical and directly significant emotional expression. This Elektra *has not the narrative continuity of* Miracle in the Gorbals, *nor the psychological interest of* Hamlet. *Its immediacy won the cheers, but it is likely to work against its durability, because the dance-invention does not, in its own right, ask for aesthetic contemplation. Instantly exciting in fact, but the scenic paintings excepted, not profitably to be thought about, as the Elektra myth demands.*

– *The Times,* 27 March 1963

In New York, in the middle of the big throw, while I was hurled down to the footlights, a woman in the auditorium screamed. It must have shaken the audience – it certainly alarmed us on stage – but mercifully I did not pay attention (I could not!) because I was in mid-air. If any of us had been distracted, there could have been a nasty accident! *NN*

HOUSTON ROGERS

In March and April 1962
the distinguished
Danish premier danseur,
Erik Bruhn,
appeared as a
guest artist with the
Royal Ballet
at Covent Garden,
partnering Nadia Nerina
in Swan Lake, Giselle
and the Flower Festival
in Genzano *duet,*
which he staged,
together with the septet
from Napoli, *as a*
Bournonville divertissement
for the company.

The Royal Ballet's guest Prince of Denmark brought out, with his considerate partnering and emotional rapport, the best in his ballerina, Miss Nadia Nerina, who responded to his challenge much as earlier Dame Margot Fonteyn had responded to Mr Rudolf Nureyev. Miss Nerina's assured Odette was matched by her exultant Odile, and her performance has never been more rewarding.

The Times, 28 March 1962

Clement Crisp

There is a sadly limited vocabulary of praise for male dancers, but it is all needed to describe the superb qualities of Bruhn as a performer. That he is a prodigious virtuoso needs no stressing: what is more worthy of notice is his stylistic excellence. He is a truly classical dancer: there is no strain, no disproportion, and the essential qualities of harmony and restraint are always present; gesture and mime are freely and nobly set out, and the dance images that he creates have physical splendour within the severe limits of the classical school. As a partner for Nerina he is a most happy choice; both have great technical resource at their command, and they have achieved a rare feat of stylistic unity. Nerina was at the top of her form: her Odette had a pearl-like radiance, her Odile a brio that never declined into vulgarity and never lost sight of the dramatic shape of the Black Swan duet. Her dancing was most subtly phrased, and characterisation was clearly placed within the choreography.

– *The Financial Times*

Richard Buckle

In the palace scene, at last, Bruhn danced; and although he was not on form, being convalescent from a leg injury, it was a joy to have a dancer of such quality in the company. Strong technique, control, good manners, and on top of all this, that absolute simplicity which is one component of greatness. He has a high, easy jump and correct line; he brightened up the otherwise rather dull variation by performing en diagonale *a series of double turns in the air ending in an* arabesque fondue, *a spectacular step learnt in Russia.*

Nadia Nerina is also a wonderful dancer. The strength of her fine feet and legs, her delirious extensions and soaring jumps are the more admirable because of her perfect placing, her timing, her line and a gift she has for conveying rapture. She is now at the height of her powers and should be seen at least once a week.

– *The Sunday Times*

HOUSTON ROGERS

The Swan Queen's entry in Act II always had to be prepared: the run on was part of a swan's flight on to the lake. Standing waiting in the wings, I always thought of a great bird coming down to land, and when you look out on to the stage from the wings it does look grey, like water. *NN*

I only once decided to show off, and if it was naughty it was also great fun. When Rudolf Nureyev did his first *Giselle* in London he caused a sensation by interpolating sixteen superb entrechat-six into the second act. It was a rare achievement but it caused dismay amongst some of the company, who could do as well but, not being guest artists, would not dare change the choreography – Madam would have been furious. One night in *Swan Lake* with Erik Bruhn, when we came to the Black Swan pas de deux, on a sudden impulse I decided to do thirty-two entrechat-six instead of the usual thirty-two fouettés. I would show our guest artist what the Royal Ballet could do, for I knew that Nureyev was in the audience watching the performance. I always liked the music for the fouettés to be slow, and the thirty-two entrechat-six fitted perfectly. Erik was absolutely amazed, and so was the conductor. And so was I, because I just went on beating sixes. If I had thought about it I don't suppose I could possibly have done them. But the audience loved it – I know I did – and so did the company. *NN*

Above and opposite Black Swan pas de deux with Erik Bruhn as Siegfried.

The ballroom scene Act III with David Blair and, right, with Rudolf Nureyev.

I never found the Black Swan pas de deux as nerve-racking as the last act *Sleeping Beauty* pas de deux, because as Odile you have the character to help you, while as Aurora you have only the choreography to rely on. During the Black Swan I used to enjoy deceiving and seducing Siegfried. As soon as Siegfried soars into the coda, musically I felt that the fouettés were beginning for me. I think that if I had known that I had to come on and do the fouettés 'cold', I would have been terrified, but Siegfried's music sets the mood for them: it is part of Odile's characterisation, and they are only a small part of the whole. I was never conscious that the audience was waiting for them, but I remember feeling that if the earlier part of the pas de deux had not been as exciting as I had hoped, then the fouettés would arouse the audience.

In *Swan Lake* I think it is the entire choreographic arrangement of the Black Swan duet that makes the fouettés as exciting as they are; within the context of Odile's bewitching of Siegried, they are the final emotional touch that dazzles him. *NN*

FLOWER FESTIVAL IN GENZANO WITH NERINA AND BRUHN

Nothing could possibly be more dazzling or more exhilarating than the combination of these soaring, spinning demi-gods.

– Richard Buckle – *The Sunday Times*

Clement Crisp

If audiences are to be dazzled by dancers, then Don Quixote *seems to be the thing – and certainly Nerina and Bruhn are the dancers to do the dazzling. The gimcrack pas de deux, raddled and bespangled like an elderly circus equestrienne, is far from the Petipa original (the Opera House version is blandly anonymous) and is more suited to the tanbark than the stage. It has gained dreadful currency of late – we have seen almost as many Kitris as we have Giselles in London – but if it is to be performed, then let Nerina and Bruhn dance it as they did last night. Miraculously they contrive to give it elegance; radiant, assured, seemingly half-amused by their prowess, they soar through this transcental study with superb aplomb. Great personal art can often redeem trash, and here we have beauty of execution and classic style of a high order, although Erik Bruhn is suffering from a leg injury that imposes a certain restraint.*

– *The Financial Times*

Mary Clarke

Nadia Nerina, since her return from North America and Russia, has been dancing marvellously at the Royal Opera House. Night after night she has astonished us by the glorious perfection of her technique. Technique is sometimes frowned upon by the pundits as if it were a vulgar accomplishment; it is supposed to be subordinated to artistry and interpretation until we are no longer conscious of its existence. Yet it has its own exhilaration and there were moments, especially in the Black Swan pas de deux, and in the Don Quixote variation, when I found myself strangely moved. Skill of this order commands a kind of awe as well as admiration.

– *The Dancing Times*

Clive Barnes

What, I wonder, is ballet's equivalent to the opera-goer who fancies canaries? Whatever it is, he would dote on Nadia Nerina. You might call Nerina the most perfect machine for dancing in the Western world, and at that surprisingly valid technical level she has all the sweetness physical perfection inevitably brings. It is true that she is much more than just the top girl in the class, and teacher's pet, yet undeniably it is the faultlessness of her dancing that first appeals, making her the rose-red apple in the eye of every well-bred ballet connoisseur.

. . . For me, at least, there are few things in the theatre more beautiful to watch than a virtuoso ballerina in full cry, accomplishing impossible things with heroic grace. Last week Nerina found her top form in this Czarist razzmatazz and her flashing, curvetting dancing gave the pimento-flavoured choreography a finesse and polish that made it glitter like one of Covent Garden's own chandeliers. . . . Nerina has all the ease and assurance, all the style and authority a dancer could wish for, so that you are left pop-eyed and chuckling at the impudence of her devastating confidence trick.

– *The Spectator*

Bruhn and Nerina in the *Don Quixote* pas de deux.

With Christopher Gable in *Cinderella*.

LAST PERFORMANCE

Sylvia was to be revived as a one-act ballet for the winter season of 1967–8; by now I was a guest artist with the company, which allowed me more time to accept invitations to dance with companies abroad, but I was delighted when Freddie Ashton asked me to dance the first performance of this new *Sylvia*. I had always enjoyed the wonderfully choreographed leaps for the huntress in Act I and the serene pas de deux in Act III. It was, in fact, to be my final role at Covent Garden, and the season would see my last performance.

I had just had my fortieth birthday, and after so many years, dancing was a way of life for me. I was working harder than ever and there seemed further challenges and excitements awaiting me as a dancer, but my husband Charles and I had been married since 1955 and we wanted to have a family. It was a heart-searching matter to decide to retire, but once I had made up my mind I felt relieved and happy, and I announced my decision soon afterwards. Sadly, the family we had hoped for was not to be. Now, several years later, I look back with no regrets. I have been given many years of artistic fulfilment and great happiness as a dancer – I have been singularly fortunate. *NN*

Clement Crisp

Sylvia *was Ashton's second full-length ballet, a loving and ingenious re-creation of one of the great Opéra successes of the 1880s. Guided by Delibes' golden score, he made it an opulent and delicious spectacle warmed by the after-glow of the Second Empire; it somehow evoked the Foyer de la Danse, the Jockey Club,* petits rats, *and the Panama Scandal, one of whose leading figures – the Baron de Reinach – was the librettist. Its faults were the faults of the scenario: entirely superficial, with a glossy exterior concealing absolutely nothing; but with the Ironsides' splendid sets matching the radiant score, it was an enchanting piece, crammed with good dances. Now Ashton has recast it in one-act mould, removing the dramatic structure surrounding Orion, and reworking the action so that it contains Sylvia's meeting with Aminta, Eros's intervention, and the happy ending with true love triumphant.*

Well, if this shortening must be, it must be; I miss the pretty complications of the story – especially the second act in Orion's cave with Sylvia leading the bacchanal – but the reduction to one scene, newly shown to us last night, makes an engaging piece and there is plenty of Ashton's choreography preserved, notably the soaring entrée des chasseresses *and the final pas de deux.*

The Sylvia was Nadia Nerina, happily returned as guest with the company. She has ever been a grand huntress, with those beautifully elastic jumps riding over the music, and brilliantly resourceful in the pizzicato variation. It was a great pleasure to see once again those boldly etched arabesques, the radiant physical presence which has set such standards of virtuosity for our dancers; as always she places a clear dramatic statement at the heart of her dancing. Aminta marked the proper début of Gary Sherwood as soloist with the Opera House troupe; it is a role whose demands are technical rather than dramatic, and Sherwood stated the dances with a nice fluency, and partnered excellently.

– *The Financial Times*, 19 December 1967

FAREWELL

At the beginning of 1969 Nadia Nerina announced that she was expecting a baby and was retiring from the stage. A tribute from Richard Buckle in *The Sunday Times* on 16 February 1969 read:

'So the glorious Nadia Nerina is to dance no more. It makes one feel very old, having watched her début at Sadler's Wells in 1946, and seen her create the role of Spring in Ashton's Cinderella *a year later. She was the most dazzling of dancers; possessing wonderful speed, strength, accuracy and control, as well as line and musical sense, she also had a range from the purely classical to* demi-caractère: *she could shine as Odette–Odile in* Swan Lake *or charm as Swanilda in* Coppélia.

Undoubtedly her greatest creation was Lise in Ashton's La Fille Mal Gardée. *This role brought out in her qualities of wit and tenderness, as well as displaying her marvellous technical gifts. To have seen her mime and dance Lise is to have realised what joy ballet can give.*

Nerina triumphed in America, in South Africa, in Europe and Russia, and brought honour to Britain. Now she is expecting a baby and has made the firm decision to dance no more. The myriad admirers of Nadia Nerina will wish that Mrs Charles Gordon may live happily ever after.'

An oil painting by Bryan Organ of Nadia Nerina, 1969.

OFF STAGE

There exists a curious one-sided familiarity between audience and dancers which springs from the public's view of the dancer on stage. We see them at their physical best; we 'know' their bodies probably better than those of our close friends; we admire the shape of their legs, the curve of neck and arms. We admire them with unusual intensity as physical specimens blessed with rare gifts of movement and expressivity on stage. What we do not know – for our own good – is the exhausted, sweat-soaked body in the wings, the tired figure straining in class and rehearsal. Dancers, in any case, live in a tight, enclosed little world, probably more clannish than in any other art; their small talk is often allusive, almost secret in its jargon and its use of foreign terms of technique. This is a world in which the public has no place, and the dancer off-stage usually seeks to keep well clear of audience and fans.

But with retirement and the easing of constant professional pressures, the dancer can be faced with a very difficult new reality of every-day life, and this – because the career is so cruelly short – when still quite young.

For Nadia Nerina 'civilian life' has been far from idle; it has meant using her gifts and energies in good causes. She has put her organising power and her integrity of purpose at the service of the RSPCA, preparing fund-raising galas and working in committee. She has shared her enthusiasm for sculpture with the public: in 1971 she donated 'Zemran', a large, stainless steel standing form by the young English sculptor William Pye, to the Greater London Council for exhibition on the South Bank where it now stands outside the Queen Elizabeth Hall. The gratitude to friends and teachers who guided her during her career is still vivid enough to take her to Leningrad on the occasion of Natalya Dudinskaya's jubilee in 1973. And the charm and humour of her Lise are as unaffectedly hers off-stage as they were on; she remains what her colleagues in the ballet always knew her to be – a generous friend, a delightful companion.

CC

REMEMBERING NADIA

Arnold Haskell

My first meeting with Nadia took place when I was a 'new boy' in the Sadler's Wells organisation. The School was temporarily housed in the draughtiest of church halls during one of the coldest winters on record. I was busy recruiting staff and seeing to the new building, difficult tasks made all the more difficult since the only office space the Wells could find for me was a corridor, also exceptionally draughty, and my desk was a chest that had belonged to Mary Kingsley, evidently a pious relic left by Lilian Baylis.

The one task that I really enjoyed was the organisation of the Saturday morning lectures for Ninette de Valois' 'second front', the new young company at Sadler's Wells. This gave me a chance to meet the dancers. They were a very remarkable group, young, enthusiastic and eager to learn; the South African contingent in particular, led by the brilliant Cranko, brought something fresh to our ranks. One especially attracted my attention. I had been asked to persuade her to change her name from the Russian-sounding Nadia Nerina to something more fitting to a member of a British ballet company.

She explained to me her reasons for her choice of name; Nerina was a South African flower and had been her mother's name. After a brief period of compromise she stuck to her guns. The

Arnold Haskell's seventieth-birthday dinner. Nadia Nerina, Dame Ninette de Valois, Yvette Chauviré, Arnold Haskell, Alicia Alonso, Galina Ulanova and Dame Alicia Markova.

average dancer would have been only too pleased to take any name assigned to her by the management, but there was nothing average about Nadia. Shortly afterwards I watched her in the fancy-dress parade at the Vic-Wells Ball and remarked to my companion: 'That girl can't lose. Look at the way she walks.' I have forgotten the costume, but not that walk. And surely enough, she won the first prize.

Her dancing then reminded me of the young Baronova in its freshness and vitality. When the company came to Bath, where I was spending a few days with my mother, the most fervent of balletomanes, she was as impressed as I was with Nadia, sent her what was to be her first bouquet in England, and gave a small party for her. From then on I became interested both in the person and the artist and saw a side of Nadia that few people knew. She was deeply interested in the work of the School, and although she had only been there for two months, she realised its important role, and whenever she earned anything from a broadcast or an article, she gave us the money to assist some needy pupil. (This was long before the days of the Endowment Fund.)

Nadia was always outspoken, possibly at times too much so for the interests of her own career, but her integrity was as absolute as her loyalty to the Company.

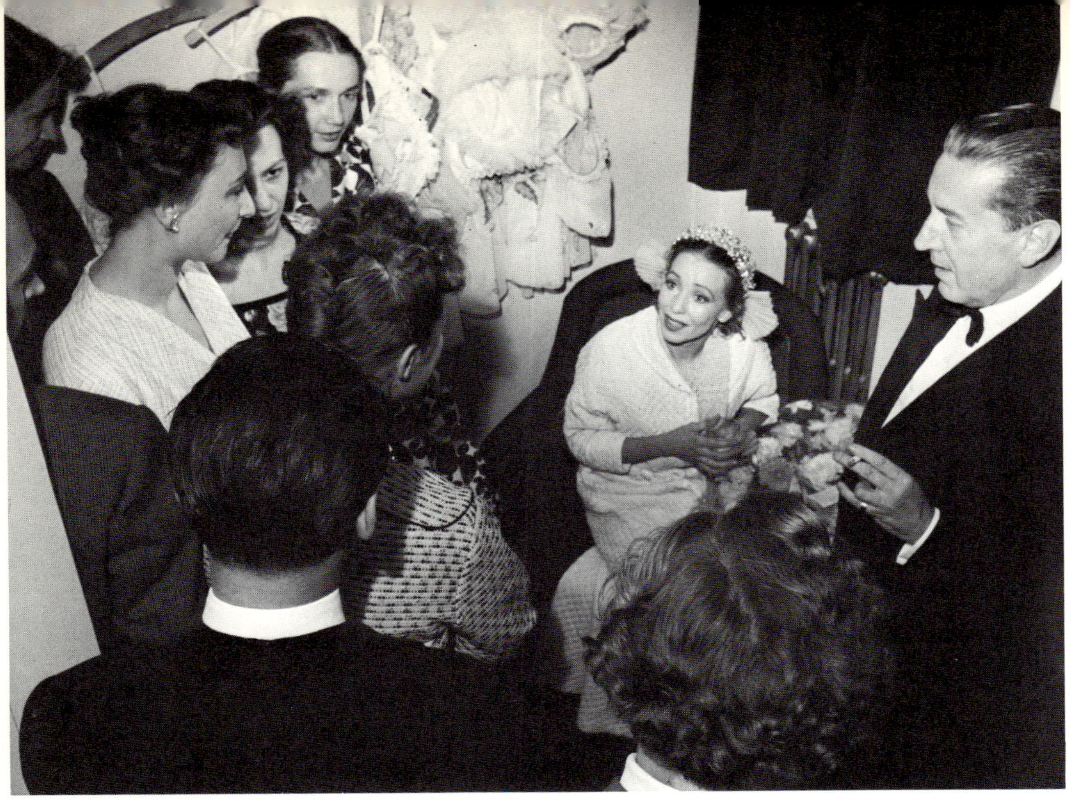

Friends from the Bolshoy Ballet visit Nadia Nerina and Sir Frederick Ashton after a performance of *Fille* at Covent Garden.

Alexander Danilova and Nadia Nerina.

What keeps dancers young is the fact that they never stop learning. In New York I took classes with Alexandra Danilova who is unchangingly beautiful, with a body of a girl of eighteen and a great sense of fun. Even then while demonstrating, her brisés were the most fantastic I have ever seen, and her classical training had given her a wonderful elegance. When she retired from dancing she gave me her make-up box, which I still treasure. *NN*

Rudolf Nureyev, Yvette Chauviré, Nadia Nerina and Erik Bruhn at the French Embassy in London.

Above Dame Ninette de Valois and Nadia Nerina in the Bolshoy Theatre, Moscow, during the company's season in Russia.
Below At Christmas time 1965, three of the Royal Ballet's Cinderellas – Margot Fonteyn, Nadia Nerina and Svetlana Beriosova – posed in the Crush Bar of the Royal Opera House wearing couture clothes of their choice, watched by the Ugly Sisters of the production, Sir Frederick Ashton and Sir Robert Helpmann, in something less than haute couture outfits. Dame Margot was dressed by Yves St Laurent, Nerina by Clive, Beriosova by Hardy Amies; the Ugly Sisters are wearing the David Walker costumes from the Royal Ballet production.

Above The presentation of 'Zemran' to the GLC. **Opposite** Nadia Nerina with her Siamese cat Nikolay named after Nikolay Fadeyechev. **Below** In 1966 Nadia Nerina presented a cast of a head of Anna Pavlova to the dance collection of the New York City Public Library. The curator, Genevieve Oswald, is seen here with Nadia Nerina, Lincoln Kirstein and Cecil Beaton.